Take Back Your
TIME

Take Back Your TIME

How to Regain Control of Work,
Information, and Technology

Jan Jasper

St. Martin's Griffin ✥ *New York*

Design by Nancy Resnick
Illustrations by Durell Godfrey

Library of Congress Cataloging-in-Publication Data

Jasper, Jan.
    Take back your time / Jan Jasper.
        p.   cm.
    Includes bibliographical references and index.
    ISBN 0-312-24334-0
    1. Time management.   I. Title.
    HD69. T54J37   1999
    650.1—dc21
                                                    99-33491
                                                    CIP

First Edition: November 1999

10 9 8 7 6 5 4 3 2 1

To my mother

Contents

Acknowledgments

This book is the culmination of a decade of work with my clients, who are a very special group of people. Changing your habits is never easy—it requires vision, risk taking, and trust. What my clients have in common is a willingness to examine themselves, to learn, to improve their skills, and continually to strive to get the most out of themselves and from life. Having such wonderful people for clients has been a great inspiration and joy, and many have become friends. In particular, I'm grateful to David Leffler, Esq., and to Ross Wisdom, C.P.A., for taking the time to read sections of my manuscript and patiently give me their feedback.

Although we've never met, the insights of authors Alan Lakein, Stephanie Winston, Barbara Sher, Marsha Sinetar, Jeff Davidson, and Barbara Hemphill have had a powerful influence on my work and my life.

I'm grateful to the National Association of Professional Organizers for getting me started many years ago and for showing me that I'm not the only one who's analytical and methodical, and that a person can actually be paid for this!

Without the early guidance and encouragement of Candy Schulman this book might never have happened. I'm indebted to Marian Faux, my book's "godmother," who introduced me to

Acknowledgments

my editor at St. Martin's Press, the skilled and wonderful Marian Lizzi. My agent, Sheree Bykofsky, is the best. The four principals of the Let's Talk Business Network—Larry Kesslin, Michael Ringel, Chris Winter, and especially Mitch Schlimer, who read and critiqued my entire manuscript—have contributed greatly through their knowledge and support.

I'm grateful to Dick and Yvonne Teske, who've helped me over the years. Susan Hansen and Carol Howell know what they've done, and I can never thank them enough. I'm blessed to have David Crystal as my best friend. And last, but certainly not least, my mother, who never fails to amaze and inspire me.

Take Back Your
TIME

Get Ready to Change Your Life

Our two greatest gifts are time and the freedom to choose—
the power to direct our efforts in the use of that time.

—STEPHEN R. COVEY

A few decades ago, experts predicted that technological advances and higher worker productivity would bring us a four-hour workday. Studies were begun to prepare the nation to cope with an expected excess of leisure. Researchers worried that the surplus of free time would lead to widespread boredom. This is as quaint to us today as a 1950s science fiction movie. We're feeling more time pressured than ever before, and it seems to keep getting worse. Complaints about not having enough time are as ubiquitous as gripes about traffic and the weather.

We are exhorted to recycle, exercise at least three times weekly for cardiovascular health, floss daily, choose the best long-distance phone company, and remember to use the discount florist coupons offered by our frequent-flyer plan. We can choose from an almost infinite number of TV channels and watch virtually any movie, new or old, in the comfort of our homes. We can have all types of cuisine prepared and delivered to our door. (Remember when your takeout choices were limited to pizza and Chinese?) We quickly get the latest information about health or investments from the Web.

In 1970 in his book *Future Shock*, Alvin Toffler predicted that we would become slaves to an overabundance of choices, thereby inhibiting action, increasing anxiety, and creating a perception of less freedom and less time. If anything, he understated the truth. We have opened a Pandora's box of too many choices, and we're paying a big price. Economist Juliet Schor notes that smarter machines and better-educated people bring more options and higher expectations. New technology reduces the time it takes to do tasks but increases the number of things we expect to do and have. Schor calls us "rich in things but poor in time."

⏱ Why Do We Feel So Stressed?

Author Jeff Davidson says that five factors are contributing to our feeling squeezed for time: population growth, the knowledge explosion, mass media and electronic addiction, the paper-trail culture, and an overabundance of choices. "Frequent-flyer programs, investments, long-distance telephone service, medical insurance, retirement options. The choices mount, the rules and regulations take longer to read, and are harder to understand." He explains, "The faster we're able to travel or to gain new

2

> information, the greater our expectations regarding what can and needs to be accomplished in our lives. We all seek to do more. . . . A day is still twenty-four hours, but it seems to shrink in the face of more to do or greater expectations about what has to be done."

While women no longer spend hours doing laundry by hand and preparing meals from scratch as their grandmothers did, they now return from the office to a second shift at home, which may include caring for aging parents in addition to the children. Downsizing has led to increased workloads and stress for the survivors—often one worker ends up doing the work of two. Many people are forced to work two or more jobs to make ends meet.

Technology: The Good News and Bad News

Technology has proved to be a double-edged sword. It has brought flexibility unimagined even a decade ago. Laptop computers and fax machines enable many people to work at home a day or two a week, avoiding the commute. Yet the same technology has eroded our personal time. That daily commute offered transition time between home and work. Only doctors and firefighters were on call on the weekend. Now our commute is interrupted by the ringing of our cell phones, and the weekend is no longer a work-free zone due to pagers and laptops. Employers and clients know that we can stay in touch from anywhere, and many of them expect it. People used to go on vacation to get away. But now, even on an ocean cruise, you can't get away—we have high-frequency radios that can send E-mail to the middle of the ocean. People on vacation in a foreign city find themselves looking for cyber-cafés to check their E-mail.

A March 1997 *Money* magazine survey found that, given the choice between taking cash or time off in exchange for working overtime, 64 percent of Americans would definitely choose the time. Americans are sleeping an average of six and a half hours per night, one full hour less than they feel they need. Many people cannot remember what it's like to feel well rested.

If you can relate to this, if you never have enough time, this book is for you. If you've read lots of time-management books and attended numerous seminars but are still suffering, this book can help you. If you feel like you're drowning, I understand. My clients often say this when they first call me for help. If you fear that your situation is worse than anything I've ever encountered, and that you're truly hopeless—sorry, I disagree. After ten years of training busy people how to function more effectively, I don't believe anyone is hopeless. If you're willing to examine where your time is going, clarify your priorities, and apply the strategies in this book, relief is on the way!

Why Is Managing Life So Difficult?

Why do so many intelligent, successful people have trouble managing their time and organizing their lives? Partly because we are not taught how when we're growing up, and what we are taught often backfires and causes more problems than it solves. For example, everyone has heard the maxim, "You should handle each piece of paper only once." Sounds good. Only problem is that it's dead wrong. Another myth: "Files should be arranged alphabetically." Maybe, maybe not. An alphabetic filing system in some cases will cause serious problems. Another piece of common wisdom: "Neatness is important." Not necessarily! People with neat desks often have ineffective work habits. The worst example of pointless tidiness I've ever seen is the method used in some offices to store incoming mail and faxes according to the date of arrival: Five folders for mail, one for each day Monday through Friday, and five more folders for faxes, again sorted by day of arrival. Standard wisdom? Yes. Effective? Far from it.

Another reason that intelligent, successful people have trouble managing their time and organizing their lives is that the world has gotten much more complicated. Even people with an innate knack for organization are hard-pressed to handle the complexity of life today. What worked ten years ago is not adequate now.

> "You can always find time to do what you want to do—if you're willing to give up something else. Life is a series of trade-offs."
> —Barbara Hemphill

Despite constant talk about how pressed everyone is for time, I contend that few people really live as if their time mattered. Most people spend more time planning their vacations than thinking about what they want to do with their lives. The way we use time is a combination of habit, the expectations of others, the influence of consumerism, and paralysis caused by too many choices. Few people use their time deliberately. We squander our time doing things because we've always done them, because other people do them, or because we're "supposed to" do them. We spend time buying more and more stuff, then spend even more time maintaining all the stuff. This is a mistake—we can always get more stuff, but *we can never get more time.* Once that really sinks in, it changes everything.

Trying to do too many things causes us to feel overwhelmed, even depressed. Most of us are familiar with "the faster I go, the behinder I get" syndrome. According to John P. Robinson, director of the Americans' Use of Time Project at the University of Maryland, the sheer number of options available to fill our time is overwhelming, whether we actually chose to do them or not. He calls this "overchoice."

Radical Time Management

My approach to time management begins with clarifying what matters most *so you can decide what to stop doing.* There's no point in getting more efficient at doing things that don't need to be done. If you think this through first (discussed in Chapters 1 through 3), you'll get maximum benefit from the time-management tips that form the bulk of this book.

For example, if you're serious about wanting to get in shape by joining a gym, you must first free up some time for it. Just buying a gym outfit and joining a gym won't do it. Unless you make time—and this may mean cutting back on TV or socializing, or working fewer hours—it's nothing but a gesture. Many people make a resolution to begin an exercise program, but they don't cut back another activity, so—not surprisingly— they don't get to the gym. Unless you can figure out how to function without sleep, you can't just keep adding things to your life. Something has got to go. Even if you won the lottery, this wouldn't change. Sure, not needing to earn a living would free up lots of time, but you'd have a new problem in its place—you'd have even more options to sort through. The most overwhelmed and frustrated people I've ever known are those who can afford to have and do everything.

Fuzzy priorities and an unwillingness to say no are what get you into trouble. They lead you to start things you can't finish, attempt too many things at once, and make promises you can't keep—all major sources of stress. Maybe you can have it all, but you can't have it all *at once*. Your first step is to start making conscious choices about how you'll spend your time and what you'll say no to. Then, with the hundreds of practical, tried-and-true strategies in this book, you will reclaim hours every week. What you do with that reclaimed time is up to you. You may just want to get out of the office at 6:00 P.M. instead of 9:00. Perhaps you want to play tennis regularly, watch your children grow up, or putter in your garden. Or you may be leading a fast-paced life and love it, yet you'd enjoy it more if you could get enough sleep.

Are You Fed Up? Great!

Anyone can learn to regain control of his or her life if there is sufficient motivation. The more fed up you are with the status quo, the better your prognosis—you'll be more willing to make the necessary changes. But it won't happen overnight. First, you make the commitment. Then you start making different choices and learn more effective ways to do things. You start to see results and get excited, which gives you the motivation to keep going. You experiment and fine-tune. Before long, time management, planning, and being organized become second nature, just like brushing your teeth. If you have a history of being "all over the place," don't despair. While you may not turn into the opposite extreme, you can modify your habits enough to get the results you want. With motivation and the tools in this book, anyone can regain control of his or her time and life.

What Does It Mean to Be Organized?

Organization is a close cousin to time management. I see them as two sides of the same coin. Being organized, though, suffers from some unflattering misconceptions. Let's debunk them now.

First of all, organization has no inherent connection with neatness, as Stephanie Winston, the country's first professional organizer, points out. Organization has no connection with cleanliness. It is not related to being perfect. (In fact, perfectionists waste a great deal of time striving for perfection in things that aren't worth the effort.) Organized people usually tend to be neat—but not always. Many neat people have terrible work habits.

A client of mine had just fired her secretary, Jane, who'd always kept her office spotless yet continually lost and forgot things. We looked in her files and found that she'd created a new folder for almost every single piece of paper. When Jane was asked to buy a picture frame, she jotted a note, dropped it into a new manila folder that she labeled "Buy Frame," and filed it in the *B*'s. Yes, she was neat—but very ineffectual.

At the opposite end of the spectrum is my friend Karen, who is too embarrassed to let me see her messy closet. I asked her, "If you have to go to an important meeting, do you show up wearing a flattering suit? Or do you frantically try on one outfit after another, finally find one that's passable, and arrive late for your appointment?" She replied, "Oh, that's never a problem. I take care of my clothes. If something needs dry cleaning, I take it right away, and I get rid of anything that no longer fits. I can get dressed in just a few minutes." I replied, "I don't see any problem. Don't fix what isn't broke!" As far as I'm concerned, Karen is organized, despite the appearance of her closet.

If being organized conjures up images of uptight, anal people who have their receipts in alphabetical order, relax. That's not what I'm talking about at all. Having your receipts in alphabetical order generally serves no purpose. (See Chapter 10, "Effective Filing," for why.) Organized people may not have spotlessly clean homes—they have better things to do.

A Means to an End

Whatever you want more of, good time management and organizing tactics will get you there. David Allen, a personal productivity consultant, says he's the opposite of a control freak. "I love being spontaneous. I love having the freedom to follow my hunches. That's hard to do when you have 473 things gnawing away at you. The reason to get disciplined and organized is not just to be disciplined and organized. It's to clear the decks so that you can operate with a broader vision."

So why all the misconceptions about what it means to be organized? It's partly because we were not taught about effectiveness when we were children. We were taught to be neat and clean, and we resented it. We were told to clean up our rooms as a reprimand, even a punishment. This is appropriate for children. But if, as an adult, you are still driven by the child inside who believes that keeping clutter around means freedom, you will have a lot of self-defeating habits. The feeling of freedom that clutter brings is only temporary. In the long run it makes you feel very stressed out.

Another residue of childhood is the feeling that being disciplined means having no freedom, as if discipline and freedom are mutually exclusive. While it may feel this way to a child, it's hardly the case for an adult. Self-discipline enables you to set your own goals and devise a strategy to reach them.

Time management and organization are not ends in themselves; rather, they're means to an end. Learning these skills will not turn you into an anal person, nor will it destroy your creativity. On the contrary—it will free you to be more creative and more spontaneous, with time to do things you never before had time for.

How to Use This Book. Mark sections that strike a chord, discuss them with a supportive friend, and perhaps start a notebook of ideas. There are no hard-and-fast rules. The right way is whatever works for you. So if you'd like to regain control of your life and, along with it, a new sense of freedom, read on.

2

Setting Priorities

There is only one success—to be able to spend your life in your own way.

—Christopher Morley

Your first step in gaining control of your life is to be brutally realistic about what you have the time and interest in doing. You won't have time to do it all. Even if you live to be one hundred years old, you *still* won't have time for everything. There will always be more things you want to do. The more things you enjoy in life, the truer this is. Even though you will save lots of time by following the advice in this book, there will still be only twenty-four hours in the day. And your days are numbered. These are facts of life. Many people prefer not to think about it, but that doesn't alter reality one bit.

The good news is that we have far more freedom than we realize. Aside from obligations like caring for children or frail elders and paying taxes, very little of what we "have" to do is morally or legally mandatory. So review everything in your life and ponder, "What's the worst that can happen if I stop doing this?" The sooner you face that your time is finite and begin to act accordingly, the less frustrated you'll feel and the more you'll enjoy life.

Reexamine Everything

Start questioning your habits. Saying no to some activities is the only way you can say yes to what you really value. Pare down what you think you "must" do. Because you've always done something isn't a good reason. At the office, skip the tasks that offer little return. Get rid of the magazines and books you don't have time to read. Stop buying every piece of software that catches your eye. At home, clean your house less often. Donate to charity the clothes that you never wear, even if they cost good money and are like new. Throw out the broken objects that you aren't willing to spend time fixing. Reevaluate the friends you've known for twenty years with whom you no longer have much in common. Maybe even get rid of your TV set. People have done it and lived!

Ah, but how about earning a living? you ask. Even here you have more options than you think you do. I know a divorced mother, now in her late forties, who has never had a full-time job. For years she has supported her family by selling her handmade pottery and clothing. Without any help from her former husband, she's paid to send both of her daughters to private colleges. She has some income from a modest house she owns, because she rents it out part of each year while she travels, which she does often. For many years she's spent a portion of each winter in New Orleans, working the Mardi Gras for both profit and pleasure. Her lifestyle may not be everyone's cup of tea, but the point is that—despite two dependents and no outside help—she did it. We have more choices than we think we do. The key is to hone in on what matters most to *you*.

Gail Blanke, a former executive at Avon Products who left to run LifeDesigns seminars, says: "A lot of women are waiting for permission, or a more convenient time than right now, to begin to live the life of their dreams—whether it's a business of their own, a new product line, a new relationship—whatever 'great' would look like in their lives. . . . Most of us are walking around in straitjackets. We have bought into a number of barriers in terms of why we can't live a life or have a career that absolutely thrills us. . . . We aren't the right person, it isn't the right time, we don't have the skills. . . . When you examine those assumptions and barriers, you find that very few exist as facts. When you can open yourself up to what would be possible, it's stunning the amount of energy you have to create breakthroughs in your life."

Making Conscious Choices

Few people habitually make conscious choices about how to spend their time. Many people will attend a concert in which they have little interest because it's free, or because someone invited them and they have no other pressing obligations at the moment. Yet, as for that pet project they've been deferring for years, they complain that they have "no time." People tend to take the course of least resistance, postponing what they want most for whatever's easiest to do now. According to Alan Lakein, the founding father of time management in the 1970s, the way we use time is primarily due to habit, a desire to escape, acting on the spur of the moment, default, responding to the demands of others, or—all too infrequently—conscious decision.

We feel the pull of all kinds of experiences we feel we should have. We feel guilty that we never get around to most of them. We hoard brochures of seminars that we don't have time to attend. We clip articles about things we shouldn't eat or more healthful ways to cook what we should eat. We collect travel brochures for places we'd like to see. But unless we're willing to sacrifice a current activity to make room to attend that seminar, saving the brochure is an exercise in self-deception. Some people buy diet books *instead* of learning to eat better. Collecting travel brochures for dozens of trips does not increase the chance you'll take any trips. In fact, when you finally do have the time and money for a vacation, you'll have so much clutter that you won't be able to find the brochures for your favorite destination. You may not even be able to find your passport!

Pretending to Do Something Versus Doing It

Collecting seminar brochures and diet books is not the same as *doing* the things they represent. Unless you start setting priorities and arranging your life around them—and that may mean jettisoning other activities to make time—you will never have time and energy actually to take the seminar or change your diet. Saving all this stuff without an action plan ultimately only increases your frustration.

Part of why we're swamped with stuff is that we buy things we don't need because they're on sale, such as the magazine subscription that begins with three free issues. Then we feel frustrated and guilty because there's no time to read them. The real problem is not that you don't have time to read them, but that you bought something you didn't really want because of a discount offer. Something in which you have no real interest does not become more valuable just because it's on sale. Acquiring things you don't need because they're cheap or free says that money counts but your time does not. The truth is just the opposite: It's your time that matters the most. *You can always get more stuff, and you can always get more money. But you can't get more time.* The more possessions you have, the more you must find a place to put, the more you have to clean, and the more you have to repair or replace eventually. More stuff means less time!

It's okay to miss a movie that "everybody" is seeing. It's okay to say no to unwanted social invitations to free up time for a pet project you've been wanting to start. Sure, you can choose to respond to peer pressure, but be aware that it's your choice. You will not be banished to the tundra to die alone because you decline an invitation. Your family will not be deprived of what really counts if you vacuum the house less often.

Do a Whole-Life Audit

Consider cleaning out your closet as a metaphor. If you take a quick glance into your closet, you might discard only two or three items. This doesn't free up much space because lots of garments you never wear remain in place. It's far more effective to take everything out of the closet, then put back only what you wear often. This leaves a great many garments you never wear because they no longer fit, are damaged, or are outdated. Get rid of them, give them to charity. You'll end up with far fewer clothes in your closet, but you'll wear more of them. Ten flattering outfits you enjoy wearing—and can get out of the closet without straining a ligament—is, practically speaking, "more clothes" than a closet crammed full of fifty outfits that you never wear.

I urge you to unclutter your life in the same way. Do an audit of your life. Notice what gives you energy and what drains you. Look at where your time goes and keep only what you must. Scrutinize your appointment book and your piles of unread magazines. Your belongings and your to-do list. The "musts" lurking in your head that you feel guilty about not getting around to. The time-saving devices that work only half the time. The projects you started but didn't finish. The friend you've known forever whose conversations are nothing but whining about his self-imposed problems.

Laura Berman Fortgang, a professional career coach, has this advice if you're feeling swamped and out of balance. "Clear the slate. Ruthlessly cut out all the things that do not directly make you money or bring you joy. Get rid of volunteer work regardless of what anyone will think. Even drop some things you like to do, just to create a little space in your life. You can always put them back later.

"Identify your top three priorities. . . . There may be peripheral needs and wants, but determine what are the three most important aspects of your life and don't let anything . . . get in their way. For example, you may choose spouse, children, and career. These are pretty huge and they do leave out things like exercise or sprucing up your golf game. That's okay. For the next year, you may let those things take a backseat until your priorities change again. We get into trouble when we want to be perfect in every area. . . .

"Say 'no' a lot. Get obligation out of your vocabulary. Stop saying 'yes' because you 'should.' Don't worry about ruffling some feathers. You have to be selfish to get balance back into your life. Only when you have more time than you know what to do with can you say 'yes' again."

Less Is More

You may feel, at first glance, that there's very little you could cut out. Most of what you want to do has some merit, which makes it hard. People with above-average interests and talents have above-average frustration. You keep the magazines because you really do want to read them; you like to be informed. You really do mean to get back to those unfinished projects. The problem is there are only twenty-four hours in the day, and you get more and more frustrated. I'm not talking here about the potential benefit, but the *actual* benefit. If you have 500 books and read only 10 of them, the benefit to you is the same as if you owned only 10 books. It doesn't matter how much life-changing information may be in the other 490 books. If you don't have time to read them, they're of no use to you. You may as well not have the 490 books. In fact, you're better off without them because of the frustration and guilt they cause—and the space they take up.

For some people it's books, for others it's clothes, self-improvement tapes, Internet sites, recipes, volunteer activities, or sports equipment. Whatever you're swamped with, attempting to do a little less is the first step toward effective time management. Saying no to some things frees up time to say yes to more important things. Trying to do everything will only make you miserable. In fact, you'll complete fewer things and enjoy them less, always feeling anxious that there's something else you should be doing instead. Letting go of some things you'd like to do is hard But it's far more painful to keep deluding yourself that it's possible to do everything—that keeps you running, like a hamster on a treadmill.

I speak from experience. I have tons of interests, and I'm a recovered clutter bug. There was a time when I couldn't resist any appealing offer: crafts, books, antiques, clothes—I was drowning in all of it. I loved to shop at yard and estate sales and couldn't resist a bargain. At times my apartment floor was so covered with my various hobbies and purchases that I could hardly walk. But that's history. Now I'm reformed. I recently declined to join a mail-order crafts-kit club and passed on joining a shoppers' discount club. Was I no longer interested in these things? No, I'm still interested. I've decided to do less so I don't feel so overwhelmed. I can live with the idea that there might be something great out there that I'll miss. There will be other offers. I've got enough on my plate already.

Hey, I even throw away offers for new long-distance calling plans. I choose not to spend my time looking at all of them. It's not worth it to me to spend that time just to save a couple bucks. But I'm very thorough about choosing health insurance—after having been forced by my former HMO to wait three months for a biopsy, I won't skimp on my health plan. I do meticulous comparison shopping and I read all the fine print. Because it's time-consuming, I'm this selective only with things that really matter. Since I stopped trying to do so much, my productivity and pleasure have skyrocketed, and my stress is far less.

> "We are in an era of seeming unlimited possibilities," says Anacaria Myrrha, a professional organizer in San Rafael, California. "We have access to more information than at any other time in history. We are exhorted to purchase, to consume, to give, to join. We are offered beauty, status, riches, pleasure (and extended life spans). Human beings are not well suited to unlimited possibilities. Living without boundaries on a daily basis produces anxiety, frustration, and insecurity. Without a clear definition of how we choose to spend our time, we fall prey to every interesting outside stimulus and are easily caught in the ebb and flow of the urgent but not important. We are spread too thin, we regularly perform crisis management, and everything never gets done. . . . When all options are constantly available, little can be accomplished in depth or with a sense of well-being, and over time, depression and exhaustion may result. When I sit with clients as they look over their lists and schedules, struggling to select their priorities, I realize that our choices are no longer between good and bad, want and don't want, or even better and best. Most of the things we want are the best, but are simply too

much and too many for a single lifetime. I have concluded that we can derive satisfaction and contentment from our lives only if we set limits for ourselves. If they arise from a value system that honors those things that fulfill us in the deepest sense of our being, they will inspire us and bring us joy. The paradox is that by choosing limits, we can experience a measure of freedom not possible when all possibilities are constantly available."

3

How Do You Want to Spend Your Time?

The truly free man is he who can decline a dinner invitation without giving an excuse.

—JULES RENARD

Traditional time-management advice is based on the premise that all you need is efficient habits. The problem is, you can be efficiently checking things off your to-do list and not even touch what really matters. Your first step, then, is to clarify what's most important to you. This is essential because we have almost limitless options today.

Time management offers us tools, but we need principles as well. We need a compass as well as a clock, according to Stephen Covey. When we talk about time management, it seems ridiculous to worry about speed before direction, about saving minutes when we may be wasting years, Covey notes. You can't use your time well unless you know what your priorities and values are. These must be set by *you*—not your boss, your spouse, your parents, your kids, social convention, or even the force of your own habits. It's much easier to spend your time in a focused way when it comes from within.

Although many philosophers over the ages have told us to look inside ourselves for guidance, most people don't. Why? Because there's no social reinforcement for doing what we really want to do. We get approval only for doing what our family, peers, and society expect of us. Many people are so used to doing what others expect them to do that they have no idea what they really want. Activities done for your own enjoyment don't count.

Take my friend Steve. I once asked him what he'd done last weekend. He said, "Nothing." I persisted, "Really, what did you do?" Finally he replied, "My wife was out of town, so I didn't do anything. I read a book, I took a walk in the country and took a bunch of photos, I cleaned up the den, I went to a concert, and I wrote some letters." Sounds to me like Steve had a pretty full weekend! Yet because they were all solitary activities, he downgraded it as "doing nothing."

Whose Life Is It, Anyway?

We carry around old shoulds from the past. *I should clean my plate. I should wash all the windows every April. I should meet others' needs first. I should never wear the same outfit twice in a week.* You're an adult now. It's time to reevaluate these shoulds.

Your parents may expect you to keep a spotless house. Advertising images tell us we should have it all, plan elaborate holiday celebrations, have large, beautifully tended yards, and be perfectly dressed and groomed all the time. You don't *have* to do any of these things. They are all voluntary. All of them!

Decide what *you* want. Be honest with yourself about why you're doing what you're doing. Do you really want the same things today that you wanted a decade ago? Are you continuing on the same old path because you fear criticism or failure if you follow your dreams?

For example, if you are active in community groups and volunteer work and constantly feel overwhelmed by the demands on your time, ask yourself, "Is this how I want to spend my time now?" If the answer is no, cut back to a level you're comfortable with (even if the level is zero involvement). If all these activities are important enough to live with the demands on your time, then stop complaining—*that's* a drain on your energy and happiness. Take responsibility for the choices you make.

Learn to Say No

Some people get their self-esteem from being needed. They need approval: They value others' opinions of them more than their own well-being. There are people who don't really want relief—they love urgency and pressure, despite their complaints. They want to think—and to convince everyone else—that they have more to do than anyone else; it makes them feel important.

Sometimes the demands of others provide us with an excuse for procrastinating about more important things we should be doing. Herb was a successful fifty-year-old psychotherapist who ached to change careers yet couldn't seem to get moving. He complained about the ceaseless demands of his relatives, yet he ignored my suggestions that he set some limits. It became clear after a while that he wanted it that way. If his family wasn't constantly coming to him with their every little problem, he couldn't blame them for not pursuing his dreams—he'd have to confront himself.

It's not healthy always to accommodate everyone else's

needs at the expense of your own. Make time for the most important people, and prune your life of people who take more than they give. We've all had people in our lives who habitually take more than they give, robbing us of emotional energy. I'm not suggesting that you jettison a friend who is in a jam and needs your help. I'm talking about the "friend" who feels free to call you at 1 A.M. when she's down in the dumps but is always too busy when you're in a jam. The acquaintance who constantly calls to pick your brain—he calls it networking—but when you call him with a request, he doesn't call you back. The aunt whose visits are nothing but unkind gossip about family members.

Many of us, especially women, were taught that to be good human beings we must sacrifice our needs to others. This isn't true. Positive selfishness—getting your own reasonable needs met—is necessary for healthy relationships. Also, you don't help others by depriving them of the chance to learn to do things for themselves. And ultimately, if your own needs aren't being met, you become too depleted to help others anyhow. You can't give to your loved ones if you are depleted, cranky, and frantic.

Learn to say no and hold your ground. If you're in the habit of putting others first and yourself last, it can be a challenge to learn to act as if your needs matter. Start with saying no to small things. (Why should you be the only one who cleans the cat box?) Then build to bigger no's. (Encourage co-workers to solve their own problems, and stop working late every day to take up others' slack.)

Laura Berman Fortgang, author of *Take Yourself to the Top*, recommends, "rubbing obligation out of your repertoire and only forming and keeping relationships out of choice. Choose to have certain people in your life, choose to let others go. . . . Why would you purposely keep people in your life who hold you back? . . . If you choose to keep these people in your life, that is your prerogative; however, ask yourself why and set boundaries to what kind of time you spend with them." As for the relationships we didn't choose, she suggests redefining difficult or draining relationships with family members to get them on a healthier, more nurturing track, rather than passively feeling victimized.

Getting Out from Under

Here's how one of my clients, Cheryl, restructured her time to reflect her priorities. In preparation for our first session, I directed her to turn her appointment book into a time log. She was to record not only appointments but also evenings spent with her son or with friends, movies or arts events she attended, time spent on household management, errands, TV, etc. At our first session she showed me around her large apartment and the formidable piles of magazines, catalogs, unread newspapers, mail, and clothes and household items in need of repair. She was very eager for me to help her sort them out and tidy up.

I told Cheryl that if we did that now, in another month or two she'd be back where she started. Instead, I had her make a list of the most important things she wants to do, as well as her obligations. Her list included: her job, which took up four days a week, finish decorating her apartment, work on the book she wants to write, investment planning, choosing a high school for her son, serving on several boards, and visiting and helping her elderly mother.

Then we looked at the time log she'd kept for the last three weeks. Besides her job, there were two board meetings, several hours spent at home on board activities, and two visits to her mother. The rest of the time was spent on social outings with friends, TV watching, or was unaccounted for. "There's nothing wrong with this if you're happy and taking care of what you need to," I said, playing devil's advocate. Cheryl repeated how discouraged she was that nothing was getting done. She confessed that she often went out or watched TV because she felt frustrated and didn't know where to start.

We went to work with her appointment book. First we filled in Cheryl's job schedule for the next six weeks. We scheduled some time for her to finish the decorating—she estimated it would take five half-days during the workweek and six full weekend days, so we picked some time slots and penciled this in. We wrote "choosing high school" and "investment planning" on three weekdays when she would not be at her job, because the required phone calls would need to be made during business hours. She wrote "Mom" on the time slots when she usually sees her mom. We scheduled several sessions to tackle her book—she chose three weekdays and one weekend when her son would be away, so it would be quiet. Then she wrote in the board activities. There was virtually no time left for leisure, not to mention basics like eating and spending time with her son.

I explained to Cheryl that the schedule we'd just created is not set in stone, but it illustrates two things: how proper planning ensures that the most important things get handled, and the grim reality of how her available time stacked up against all the things she wanted to do. She decided to get off two of the boards to free up time for other things. She also resolved to clear out her junk and finish decorating her apartment—once she felt comfortable at home, she could concentrate on writing her book.

Now we were ready to tackle Cheryl's piles of magazines, catalogs, unread newspapers from last month, seminar and cultural event listings, and clothes and household items needing repair. Her attitude was very different from an hour before. She no longer was content just to "straighten things up." She started throwing things out like crazy. Papers were flying into the recycling bin, and she filled a big bag with items to give to charity. She lingered over a huge pile of clipped articles she'd planned to mail to friends, saying, "I'm always behind—some of these I clipped out months ago." I asked, "After you mail articles to your friends, do they thank you?" She said soberly, "One friend does, but the others never mention it." Out went most of the clippings! Having realized that she had time for only one class this fall, she selected one course catalog and discarded the other six. Her intitial reluctance had turned to relief. Cheryl said as we finished the session, "Less really *is* more. I'm starting to feel like I can breathe again!"

Making the Right Decisions

You're already setting priorities each day without thinking about it. You do it when you have four phone messages and decide which call to return first. Other decisions you postpone, and they pile up. Next thing you know, there's a huge backlog. Indecision causes things to pile up. The trick is to become aware of these "decision points" and make decisions sooner. If you have a lot of interests, you'll have to pass on some worthwhile activities to make room for those that are even more important.

Attending a concert may be "good" for Joe, a music lover whose doctor has told him he needs to relax more. But that same concert is not "good" for Bill, an aspiring concert pianist, who finds it all too easy to sit in the audience when, to reach his goals, he's better off practicing for his own performance next month.

A bestselling book may be a "good" book for Jane, but for

Sue, who needs to spend time tracking down information on her child's illness, that "good" book is a waste of time. When Jane finishes the book and enthusiastically offers to loan it to Sue, she accepts it. Why not, Sue thinks. It doesn't cost me anything, and I'll read it—someday. Yet the book gathers dust in Sue's living room, and every time she sees it, she feels frustrated. When Jane asks Sue how she's enjoying the book, she apologetically says she hasn't even opened it.

This is a minor daily occurrence, but it's worth looking at. Why should Sue apologize for having her priorities straight? Her only mistake was accepting the loan of the book in the first place (she knew she wouldn't have time to read it). Seeing the book gather dust in her living room makes her frustrated, and now she needs to explain to her friend why she hasn't read this wonderful book. It would have been better to politely turn down the proffered book: "No thanks, I won't have time to read it anytime soon." This may seem like a niggling point, but it's very important—it is a decision point that could have saved time and peace of mind. A person who's clear on what's important to her does not feel as if she has to do everything and does not apologize because she cannot. We have the opportunity to make such choices many times each week. If we make them consciously, we'll have far less clutter in our lives and be far less frustrated.

Having to pass on some worthwhile activities makes us feel sad. But there's something far worse—continuing to delude yourself that it's possible to do everything and becoming more and more exhausted and frustrated. You won't get it all done because you won't live forever. The sooner you face this, the sooner you can begin to make conscious decisions about what you will spend your time on. Believe me, it feels much better than pursuing that illusion of endless time.

Voluntary Simplicity

If you want the trappings of success, the long hours you have to work is only the beginning. You must also spend most of the time you're not working commuting to and from work, recovering from work, buying suitable clothing for work, entertaining people from work, etc. This leaves very little time for yourself or your family. It's amazing how much of our "leisure" time we spend doing things we don't want to do. The more complicated your lifestyle, the truer this is.

There are people in high-powered jobs who work on Sundays and love it—or love the income and perks it brings—so much that it's worth it. There's nothing wrong with that. But an increasing number of people are deciding that a high standard of living and a high quality of life are two different things. They've decided to simplify their lives—work less, spend less, and live more. Simplifying your life is not about self-denial and penny-pinching. Quite the opposite: It's about focusing on what matters. It's about spending less time and energy on things you don't enjoy and making room for whatever you find fulfilling.

Elaine St. James has emerged as the spiritual leader of the simplicity movement. Her four books, starting with *Simplify Your Life: 100 Ways to Slow Down and Enjoy the Things That Really Matter,* have together sold more than 1.4 million copies. She says, "Because we want to have all this stuff, we work longer to pay for it. . . . And stuff doesn't just cost money. It also takes up time—for all that installing, fixing, maintaining, listening, and watching. And what does everyone say they really want? More time! The irony is so profound."

After a successful career in real estate, St. James reexamined and changed her life. She and her husband decided that rather than adding a cook to their staff of household help (they already had a gardener and a bookkeeper), they'd simplify their lives. "We got rid of possessions that we didn't use but that took up space. We moved into a smaller home. We made changes in our social lives, our volunteer schedules, our finances, and eventually our careers. The less we took on, the more time we created." She also cut back her work schedule by two hours a day, with no loss in productivity. The couple estimates that they've each created an extra thirty hours per week.

She explains, "There are lots of reasons why people aren't doing what they want to do. For one thing, many of us don't know what that is. . . . If you've spent years not knowing what you want to do—in your career, in your family life, with your civic obligations—it can seem like an impossible challenge to figure it out. For many people, it's easier to keep doing what they know they don't want to do, or what they don't mind doing. Simplifying your life frees up time for you to figure out what really matters."

Your Money or Your Life

Even if voluntary simplicity is not for you, it's still useful to view the cost of material things in terms of how many hours you must work to pay for them. Take your income and divide by the number of hours you work in a year to arrive at the purchasing power of an hour of your time. Do you want that new sweater enough to give up five hours of your life just to have it? There will be other sweaters, but those five hours, once spent, are gone forever.

Paying cash is kissing those hours good-bye, but using credit cards is even worse, unless you pay off your balance every month. It's tempting to pay with plastic to eat in a restaurant, but when you realize that you could still be paying for that meal five years later, suddenly you lose your appetite.

Without going to extremes of frugality, you can make moderate cutbacks to get some time back. Have your family put everything they want to buy on a list and review the list in a month. See how many items fade from importance—some families can discard the whole list. When your to-do list is overwhelming, see how many low-priority items you can cross off. Stop regarding every social invitation as an obligation. Terminate subscriptions to magazines you don't read. Don't buy so many gadgets.

If you want to simplify your life, here's how:

- Slash personal spending and use that found money to pay off debts, including your mortgage, as quickly as possible.
- Reduce home maintenance by replacing your high-maintenance flower bed with a rock garden.
- Consider moving to a smaller home.
- Get rid of all the gadgets you never use. The less you own, the less to walk around, clean, find a place to put, and repair.
- If you can work at home, you save on commuting costs, wardrobe costs, and lunch costs, and perhaps child care too.
- Instead of paying a baby-sitter, trade baby-sitting with friends and neighbors. Be creative—you can trade baking for home repairs.
- Buy children's clothes and toys at yard sales.
- Buy clothes at thrift stores.
- Buy low-maintenance clothing.
- Buy used cars—no payments, lower insurance costs.

- If you live in an area with good mass transit, get rid of the car. Spared that expense, you can pay off your mortgage sooner.
- Share garden tools, lawn mowers, etc., with neighbors.

New Year's Resolutions

You've probably made New Year's resolutions. And you've probably noticed that they last about a week. New Year's resolutions fail because they're based on what you think you should do, not what you really want to do. To be effective, a resolution must be heartfelt—and backed with an action plan. Figure out what you really want—the goal behind the goal—and plot out a realistic method of getting there. For example, you may feel you should exercise, yet you can't force yourself to do it. But your underlying wish is to be fit and have more energy. Spending hours on the treadmill is not the only means to this end. Perhaps you could better accomplish this by taking up biking or tennis. It would be more fun, so you could stick with it—and you'd achieve the same result.

Another thing that shoots down New Year's resolutions is lack of preparation. Resolving to do things without knowing how to overcome the obstacles is futile. If you knew how, you'd have done it already. Identify what you need to learn and think through how to overcome any obstacles.

Once you've clarified what you want to do, set a deadline, figure out the steps using backward planning, and enter them into your day planner (see Chapter 4, "Powerful Planning"). Then, every day, spend at least a few minutes on activities related to your goal. Warning: Don't set too many goals for the same time period—it's self-defeating.

Workaholism Reexamined

There are widespread misconceptions about the lifestyle known as workaholism. While many people are unhappy with demanding careers, some people thrive on it and are not harming themselves at all. For some years now, research has been telling us that workaholism is not necessarily unhealthful. Let's hear what the experts have to say.

According to Marcia Miceli, professor at Ohio State University, some workaholics "enjoy their work, have high standards, and are willing to put forth effort to obtain excellence . . . they are not dependent or obsessed with work. They are high performers who choose to continue working to pursue personal achievement. They probably don't suffer from the stress and anxiety that other workaholics do. . . . The biggest problem for achievement-oriented workaholics may come if they are pressured to spend more time in non-work activities. People are always told to find a 'balance' between work and non-work roles, but that may not be healthy for everyone. It may be more beneficial to help achievement-oriented workaholics find ways to spend more time doing what they enjoy—working."

In her book *Workaholics: Living with Them, Working With Them,* Dr. Marilyn Machlowitz concludes that workaholics tend to be healthier and happier, and to live longer than others. Workaholics don't suffer as much as those around them.

In *Do What You Love, the Money Will Follow,* Marsha Sinetar says, "On the surface, there are similarities [between someone who loves his work and a workaholic], but at the heart of each work style resides a completely different set of attitudes and motivations. The person who loves his work is drawn magnetically to that work, as if there were a pull or a perfect fit between it and himself. . . . On the other hand, the motivation of a 'workaholic' is usually fear. . . . [He] typically uses work to stave off buried hostility, maladaptive social attitudes, and feelings of inadequacy."

According to Pepper Schwartz, professor of sociology at the University of Washington, some very busy working parents are actually quite happy, especially when they like their jobs and get satisfaction from all their roles.

Type A Reexamined

On a similar note, recent research on the type A personality has found that—contrary to the earlier belief—being driven, competitive, and impatient isn't in itself dangerous to health. It's only when coupled with hostility, antagonism, and mistrust (versus productivity and fulfillment) that it's dangerous.

In short, if you feel exhilarated by your work and you take care of yourself, you're not a workaholic. But if you use work to avoid dealing with internal or external problems—that's a different story. The point is to figure out what *you* want and not let anybody else tell you.

Rather than trying to make a few timid changes, I recommend that you boldly examine how you spend all your time. Do what Cheryl did: Make a list of what's most important to you and then consider where your time's currently going. You may have to make some tough decisions. Once you've decided where you want to focus your time, the following chapters will give you plenty of nuts-and-bolts tools for making it a reality.

4

Powerful Planning

Nothing is particularly hard if you divide it into small jobs.

—HENRY FORD

If you think you don't have time to plan, you've got it backward. You don't have time *not* to plan. *The reason you don't have time is because you don't plan.* People who don't plan move from one crisis to another. Once planning becomes habitual, most crises are nipped in the bud. A few minutes of planning will save you many hours of wasted effort. Planning is especially important for people who often race around at the last minute to meet deadlines. Planning can prevent this. If you often worry that there's something else you should be doing but you forget what it is, planning will help you, too.

If you keep an appointment book and a to-do list, you may wonder what else there is to know about planning. The answer is—a lot! For most people, appointment books and to-do lists are nothing more than lists of minutiae. This approach barely scratches the surface.

Effective planning starts with the realization that some activities have higher payoffs than others. The most important things in our lives are often not urgent, they don't require immediate attention. Getting a medical checkup, drawing up a will, setting up a retirement saving program—despite their obvious importance—are easy to postpone. They aren't urgent—yet. But by time they become urgent, it's too late. The solution is to use your appointment book to schedule time to make sure you take care of these things in advance. Make a note to call your insurance agent to review your policies. Make an appointment with yourself to do the necessary research to create a living will. Don't just add it to your to-do list—assign it a time slot!

This is the opposite of what most of us do. Our time is taken up by the immediate and pressing, and we hope that "someday" we'll have more free time to tackle the big stuff. Of course, unless we actively make time, "someday" never comes. And until you take charge, it will only get worse: The longer you go on not dealing with the big-picture things, the more of your time will be lost dealing with the crises that result. It's a vicious cycle. The way to break this cycle is to schedule time for important things that require an investment of time now but pay off handsomely later. It takes a little effort, but it repays you many times over. If you think you're too busy to do this, you're confusing activity with productivity.

The Four Quadrants

Stephen Covey's Four Quadrants paradigm is extremely useful. Covey clarifies the relationship between urgent and not urgent, the important and unimportant. Quadrant One is the urgent and important, such as meeting an imminent deadline or undergoing heart surgery. Clearly, these must be tended to immediately. Quadrant Two is the important but not urgent— yet. Because it's not urgent, it's easy to put off. It includes preparation, prevention, planning, true re-creation, and rela- tionship building. It includes the planning that enables you to meet deadlines with ease. It includes the attention to your health that makes heart surgery unnecessary. The more time you spend in Quadrant Two, the less time you spend in Quad- rant One because things have been handled before they become crises. Quadrant Three is the urgent but unimportant. These *seem* urgent because they consist of phone calls, meet- ings, and drop-in visitors—in short, meeting the expectations of others. These activities have some value, but less than it appears. Quadrant Four is activities that are neither urgent nor important; Covey calls it the Quadrant of Waste. It includes mindless reading and TV watching and gossiping. It masquer- ades as recreation, but it's not true re-creation. We do it to help us cope, but it's deterioration more than survival, Covey says. Quadrant Four is where we escape to when we're exhausted from Quadrants One and Three.

The solution is to spend more time in Quadrant Two, attending to the important but not urgent. We've seen how this minimizes time spent responding to Quadrant One emer- gencies. When your time is filled with high-priority, high- payoff activities, you're focused enough to stave off many Quadrant Three activities, and Quadrant Four escapism sim- ply holds little appeal.

How to Plan

Most people plan from the wrong end. Planning doesn't mean listing tasks to get you through each day, doing the same for the next seven days to make your week, and then you do that every week and you've got the year. It's just the opposite. What you want to accomplish by the end of the year determines what you need to do this month. What must be done by the end of the month tells you what should be done next week and this week. What you should do today and tomorrow depends on what must be done next week. So, start with what you want to accomplish this year, break it down into pieces, and work backward.

Backward Planning in Action

It was June, and my client Andy anticipated a busy fall of fundraising for his nonprofit institute, leading up to the big annual conference in November. Even though his assistant had just left without warning, Andy was in high spirits. He was looking forward to going away for the entire summer. He planned to do the June issue of the newsletter just before his departure. I was concerned because, without his assistant, his membership and donor records were in disarray. But, Andy said, very little could be done before fall, so this didn't affect his summer plans. Confirmations from conference speakers would not arrive until after Labor Day, and the printing and mailing of the programs depended on that. So he planned to take the summer off as usual and work really hard in September.

I pointed out that getting the membership and donor records in order might take longer than expected. Andy had to hire and train a new assistant before he could update the mailing list, and mailing the conference invitations depended on this. Cutting his time too close could have serious consequences. He'd confided that if he didn't get a good turnout at the November conference, the institute might have to fold.

Triage

So we made a list of what had to be done, estimating how many days each would take, allowing time for the normal errands, family things, etc. He realized that, even though most of the big stuff didn't have to be *finished* until November, if he waited until September to *begin* there simply wouldn't be enough time. He also saw that there weren't enough days to produce another newsletter issue and leave for vacation when he planned to. We decided he'd find a new assistant and get the institute's membership and donor records straight during the summer. To have time for that, he'd have to skip the newsletter's summer issue. True, this could cost him some revenue, but it would cost him far more if the fall conference was not top-notch. He also decided to shorten his vacation to one month. Of course he was free to take the entire summer off and risk the Institute's survival. The point is, had he not thought it through in advance, by the time he realized what his choices were, it would have been too late.

Anything—no matter how big or amorphous—can be broken down into a series of tasks, then scheduled into your appointment book. Once the important things are scheduled in advance, it's easy to guard your time against the unimportant creeping in. There's another advantage to planning: Once you've mapped out a plan of action, you can keep moving forward regardless of your mood. Rather than waiting for inspiration to strike, you need only follow the steps you've already laid out. Days when you feel low can be as productive as "good" days.

If you're stuck on how to begin a complex task or plan a project, authors Merrill and Donna Douglass suggest that you break it down in to its component parts. If you try to think of every step in sequence, you'll get stuck. You keep thinking of things later that need to be added to the list, forcing you to rewrite the list many times. Worse, if you don't know what the first step is, you don't start the project at all.

Try this method instead: Write the steps down as they come to mind—don't worry yet about the sequence—on index cards or sticky notes so you can move them around. Figure how many days or weeks each step requires and note this on each card. Then put the cards into sequence. You'll see interrelationships such as two tasks that must be done simultaneously. If any steps are missing, add them now. When you have all tasks in the proper sequence, write the big deadline on the last card, and work back in time, counting the necessary days or weeks. This tells you when you must start. Set interim checkpoints to help you stay on track. Your last step is to transfer the deadline, interim checkpoints, and tasks to your planner.

Anything you want to do can be broken down into parts in this manner. Count back from the deadline and schedule the steps into your planner. There will be changes along the way, but you'll come out way ahead compared to not planning at all. Be generous in your time estimates. Allow for unanticipated problems and additional work that will be generated along the way. Be realistic. Set goals you can meet so you won't get discouraged.

Update and fine-tune your plan as needed. Plan your workweek in advance, preferably Thursday afternoon. (Don't wait till Friday, because if you need to make important phone calls, you risk not reaching people until Monday.) Then do daily updates, either first thing in the morning or last thing in the evening. Even when you get busy, you can still do at least one small task each day toward your goals. Seeing slow but steady progress will keep your morale up.

> ### 🕐 Goals
>
> Plan to do a little more than seems realistic; if you aim high you'll accomplish more by stretching yourself. Put your goals in writing. Share the ideas with a supportive friend to whom you'll be accountable and do the same for him or her. Read your list of goals daily before you plan and before you go to sleep.

Make Planning a Way of Life

Now you've got the concept of how to plan. But where to write it all down? Believe it or not, in your appointment book or planner. If you use it only for meetings and doctor appointments, you're cheating yourself. Your planner is control central for your whole life. That's why I prefer the term "planner" to "appointment book."

Keep your planner handy at all times; take it with you everywhere. One of the most effective people I know takes his planner into the sauna at his gym! Use the same planner for work and home; otherwise you're in trouble. If you have children, you'll also want to keep a family activities calendar in the kitchen. (See Chapter 15, "Home and Family.")

Write appointments in pencil. This makes it easier to keep your planner updated and looking tidy. (I've noticed that when people use ink, the ugly cross outs that result seem to deter them from using their planner faithfully.) When you make an appointment, note the person's phone number next to the name in the time slot. This makes it easier to contact the person if you have a change of plans.

Choose Your Planner Carefully

A planner must meet two criteria: In addition to spaces for appointments, it must have plenty of blank space for miscellaneous reminders. Second, you must be able to see an entire week at a glance. Don't buy a planner that shows only a day at a time—it'll cause problems because you can't see the big picture. A month at a glance format makes it even easier to see the big picture, but it has very little space for each day. A week-at-a-glance format is the best of both worlds—it gives you room to write, yet you can see the month easily by turning only four pages, one page per week.

While there are many planner formats available, there are only two that meet these criteria: Planner Pad ($19.95–$24.95, available only from Planner Pads, Inc., 5088 S. 107 St., PO Box 27187, Omaha, NE 68127-0187; 402-592-0676). Also good is the Quad Planner ($21.65, from your local office supply store or directly from the manufacturer, At-A-Glance Company, 607-563-9411; ask for item #7839005).

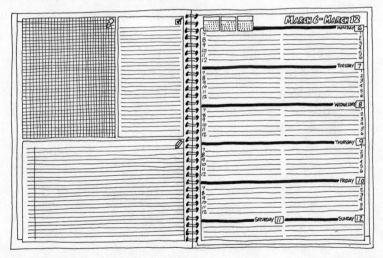

The Planner Pad from Planner Pads, Inc.

The Quad Planner from At-A-Glance

The Planner Pad is ideal. It combines the standard calendar and dated to-do lists with blank sections at the top of each page that you can label for the major areas of your life. A parent who's remodeling the house, is active in community affairs, and is on a health program could label the columns Family, House, Community, Health. If your primary focus is your career, you could dedicate a column to each client or project. Regardless of how you use the columns, they help you plan ahead, and seeing what's checked off provides a quick overview of a project's status.

Your planner isn't just for appointments. You can use it for notes about all kinds of things.

- To remind you to do something in a specific window of time. You want to attend the marketing seminar next month but won't know if you're free until the 20th. The deadline for registration is the 22nd. So you mark your planner to register the 21st.
- Follow-up calls to clients.
- Your medical test results should be back Thursday. Jot down "Call doctor Thursday for results."
- Reminders of things to bring along: meeting notes, a client's file, the book you want to loan to a friend, theater tickets, directions to a dinner party.
- If you forget to back up your computer files, mark it down as a weekly task.
- You've decided to expand your circle of friends. Set a quota of calling one person per week whom you'd like to have coffee with.
- Your son needs his doctor's written okay for summer camp. This form must be mailed by May 31. Write it down.

- You want to go to the gym but never have time. Make an appointment! If you need to buy new sneakers first, make an appointment for that, too. How about Thursday during your lunch hour?
- Carl said he'd get back to you by Monday and you're in trouble if you don't hear by Wednesday. Make a note "Heard from Carl?" on Tuesday morning.
- Due dates on major bills you must pay.
- Dates that family, friends, or clients leave on and return from trips. This way you won't schedule a late meeting the evening before your spouse leaves town.
- Events you need to be aware of even if they don't require your presence. Sharon, who owns a training company, notes her company's training schedule so she knows which classes are going on when.

Circle any deadlines, presentations, or weekend guests. You can see at a glance when these big days are and can allow the necessary time to prepare. This way you won't overload yourself. Try to leave the day before a trip or major deadline clear to give you time to prepare, then give yourself another day after to catch up. (This is an example of why the week-at-a-glance format is superior to the day-at-a-glance format.)

Those loose ends we usually leave until the last minute—or don't get to at all—can be planned, too. You probably don't write these in your planner because scheduling a time seems too rigid. Here's a method that enables you to plan yet stay flexible. Write down tasks whenever you think of them, but don't write them in your planner directly. Write them on a sticky note first, then move them to your planner later. Your loose ends might include "take clothes to dry cleaner," "buy shoes for Suzie," "Dad's birthday gift," "review insurance policy," "resume playing tennis," and "waterproof basement." Jot each of these on a separate sticky note.

When you sit down to plan your week, you realize that you'll drive right past the dry cleaner on the way to Suzie's dentist appointment, so you put the dry cleaner sticky note on that day. (You'll see this the day before the dentist appointment, so you'll gather the clothes the night before rather than wait until the last minute.) If you want to switch insurance policies, you'll have to decide before your current policy expires. You want to talk to a knowledgeable friend first, and you decide to call him Tuesday. You write this directly in the planner and discard the sticky note, because this can't wait. Since Suzie has to be with you to try on shoes, you move the sticky note for shoes to the time slot after her dentist appointment. (If Suzie must have new shoes right away, write it in the planner right after "dentist" and discard the sticky note.) To resume playing tennis, you must first have your tennis racket restrung. You create a note for "have racket restrung" and stick it onto Wednesday after work. To waterproof the basement you'll first need to get names of reputable contractors. If you want the basement done before winter, you'd better start calling contractors in late August. Stick the "calls for waterproofing basement" note in that week. This takes care of everything except Dad's birthday gift, which you leave stuck in the margin of next week in your planner. You'll move it to the appropriate time when you see how the week shapes up.

Look for opportunities to kill two birds with one stone. If you want to exercise and also spend time with your daughter, you could go hiking or swimming together. If you want to take a class but long to see your best buddy from college more, invite him to take the class with you.

Put a note in the front of your planner saying that if it's

found, you offer a reward for its return. One advantage of using software is the ability to create backups, which is the best way to keep your data safe. The principles are the same as those given here for paper planners. (See Chapter 11, "Taming Technology.")

The next chapter shows how a functioning desktop and your day planner work together to help you get things done.

🕐 A Place to Capture Ideas

Often we think of things we might like to do someday, but we're not ready to make a commitment, so it doesn't make sense to add them to our to-do list. But if we don't write them down somewhere, we'll forget. One solution is to keep a notebook where you capture your ideas. Whenever you think of something you want to do "someday," write it in your notebook. Jot down project ideas, gift ideas, films you want to rent, miscellaneous ideas, and even what you'll serve and whom you'll invite to your next party. Divide your notebook into sections and label the tabs by areas of your life (family, leisure, career, books and movies, etc.). You can add your own adhesive tabs if you need to. Jotting it here is not a commitment, just a way to remember. Then when you do your weekly planning, flip through your notebook, pick out what appeals to you, and transfer it to your planner.

While this is great for the short run, bear in mind that if you make this a habit, eventually you'll have dozens of these notebooks and you won't be able to find anything. There are three ways to avoid this problem. When you're ready to act, tear out pages and transfer them to the appropriate project file (see Chapter 10, "Effective Filing"). Stick to one topic per page, and don't write on the backs. When you've filled one book, go through it from the beginning, tear out any pages that are still relevant, file them as needed, and discard the book. A second solution is to keep all notebooks intact for posterity but add indexes to make them manageable. Leave blank several pages in the front when you start a new book and build the index there as you go along. This takes more time, but it works well for people who like to keep old notebooks in chronological order. The third way to keep your information accessible is to replace the paper notebook with the computer! You can do word searches to quickly locate things. (See Chapter 11, "Taming Technology.")

Reality Check

Monitoring where your time is going will help you allocate it properly. Grab some highlighter pens and your planner, assign a color to each major area of your life, and mark every item accordingly; for example, yellow for health, green for career, blue for family. Mark in yellow your stints at the gym, yoga class, smoking cessation support group, doctor checkup, and your visit to the department store to check out the home tread-mills. Mark in green your networking breakfasts, presentations you'll give, seminars you'll attend, and training sessions with your speech coach. Continue for the other areas. If you place equal value on improving your health and advancing your career, yellow and green should be balanced. But if you've worked yourself into a stress-related illness and you want to put your health above your career, and you see that your day planner is full of green and very little yellow—that's a wake-up call.

Planning Board

If you need to have things spread out in front of you so you can think, you're not alone. Here's an excellent planning system for visual people. Brad Swift, life purpose coach and founder of the Life On Purpose Institute, has developed this system for "life management." He and his wife use an "action and results board," which is a three- by four-foot bulletin board on a prominent wall in their office. It's divided into sections reflecting the major areas of their lives: his writing career; her nutritional supplement business; their rental property; their goal to live a simple, debt-free lifestyle; their Life On Purpose Institute; family projects; and volunteer work. At the beginning of each month they spend two hours updating the board. They assess the previous month's accomplishments and decide what results they want for the upcoming month. They write these desired results in each category; below that, they list the specific actions they'll take. Then, at the start of every week, they look at the board to see what they will be working on. Brad says, "Our ability to accomplish our goals sky-rocketed when we started to manage them this way. Those two hours we spend planning are some of the most productive time we spend the entire month. Many people are amazed at how many different things we are involved in, yet we still have time for such important matters as taking our seven-year-old daughter, Amber, to the pool."

You Can Take It with You

If you want to make use of spare bits of time during the day, carry the following with you (if you use a paper planner you can keep this in the planner's pockets or binder): your bank account number and deposit slips, family members' clothing sizes, errands list, phone numbers of repair people, and medical insurance information. If you're active in an organization, keep members' phone numbers and notes about upcoming events so you can return calls promptly. The more uses you find for your planner, the more you'll be prompted to turn to it. Soon it will become second nature.

Caution: Many people transfer their desktop clutter to their planner and lug it with them everywhere. I've seen planners that weigh twenty pounds! Don't stuff your planner with papers and leave them there indefinitely. The only papers inserted into your planner should be the things you need today—directions to this afternoon's seminar, a party invitation for this evening. Information for a seminar six weeks away doesn't belong in your planner, it belongs in your action files (see Chapter 5, "Managing Your Desktop").

Managing Your Desktop

Your ability to achieve goals is directly related to your willingness to use the wastebasket.

—BARBARA HEMPHILL

If you're like most people, cleaning up your desk brings only short-lived satisfaction. It feels great at first, but before long you're back where you started—buried in paper. You may think it's because you got busier at work, or because you have messy habits. But that's not it. The reason your desk doesn't stay clear is that you don't have a system for managing the paper that keeps arriving. This chapter will show you how to clear your desk and, more important, create a lasting system and the habits to keep it clear.

Take a look at that mess on your desk right now. Go through every single item. Throw out junk mail and any paper that's clearly obsolete. Remove any books and magazines you never refer to (more on this in Chapter 9, "Surviving Information Overload"). Set aside reference papers to be filed. Reference papers shouldn't be on your desktop unless they are in use for a current project, in which case they deserve their own file folder (more on that later in this chapter). Designate a bin or table near the door for things to take out (letters to mail, film to be developed, things to take home).

How about the 27 sticky pads, 18 pens, 5 legal pads, 296 paper clips, and 3 pairs of scissors? Oh, and the 6 bottles of white-out that you haven't used since you got your computer? If you must hoard office supplies because otherwise your officemates will snatch them all, okay, but don't store them all on your desk or in the top drawer. Keep what you're using close at hand and store the rest of the stash in your credenza.

Now all that remains on your desk is paper you need to have close at hand because it's in process, one way or another. If it all pertains to one project that you're currently working on, it's not clutter. But, all too often, the desk is littered with unrelated papers mixed together. Perhaps the entire surface of your desk has become a giant In box. We fear that if we don't put these papers where we can see them, we'll forget them. The problem with the "leave it out in plain sight" method is that yesterday's urgent tasks get buried by today's mail, and tomorrow you place another pile on top. Next thing you know, those urgent reminders are buried and forgotten anyhow. No wonder you live with the fear of forgetting something important!

Turning Your Desk into a Pleasant Place to Do Work (Not Store It)

It *is* possible to reclaim your desk as a work surface without forgetting what you need to do. The solution is action files (some folks call them working files or hot files). They have an entirely different purpose from reference or archival files, which are used less frequently (see Chapter 10, "Effective Filing"). Action files are for current activities or pending matters only. They must be kept very close at hand, ideally in a desktop file holder.

Let's walk through the creation of action files, using Tom's desk as an example. (These work in tandem with the tickler file—see below for details.) A New York psychotherapist with a thriving practice, Tom has numerous interests. His big project is to move cross-country within the next couple of years, which requires many phone calls to check into housing prices and professional prospects in different locales, visits to cities where he might like to live, and much more.

Tom started by discarding the junk mail and everything that was clearly outdated. Then we set aside anything he needed to save but not act on, so he could file it later in his reference files—professional articles, client notes, canceled checks, an explanation of his health insurance coverage.

Everything that remained on his desk required action or pertained to current projects. Tom had a good reason to leave these papers out, but they needed to be in better order. There were articles about cities he wanted to look into, bills to pay, a dry-cleaning ticket, two party invitations, bylaws of a committee on which he served, an article he wanted to mail to his daughter, catalogs containing items he'd ordered or wanted to order, three offers for discount long-distance phone service, and a big stack of unread professional journals. So far, not bad.

But as we continued, it turned into an archaeological dig. We found receipts for tax-deductible expenses for two years ago—too late to use them now! And there was that credit card bill with an error he'd wanted to correct—the ninety-day time limit had long since passed. Tom sighed in frustration, remembering that he'd left this bill on his desk so he wouldn't forget. Book club invitations, lecture and film schedules several months old, last year's reminder to schedule a dental checkup, invitations to professional conferences he missed eighteen months ago, sale flyers for stores, some of them no longer in business. As we finished the excavation, Tom found several compact disks he'd borrowed from his brother. He'd sworn to him that he'd returned them long ago, so now he owes his brother an apology! He carefully pried them loose—they were stuck to the desk by old coffee spills and the force of gravity.

Create Folders Based on Next Actions

We grabbed a couple dozen file folders and began to file everything based on the next action required. Not where it came from, not what it is—these are not specific enough to be useful. Think of the *next action* called for. Sometimes this is obvious—a bill needs to be paid. But what about that brochure about a class Tom might want to attend, which has sat on the desk for weeks? He didn't file it because then he'd forget to sign up for the class. But he was not even sure he wanted to attend—he had to make a phone call for more information. The key term here is "phone call," because that's his next action. We made a

Phone Calls file to hold this and any other reminders about phone calls, as he'll always have phone calls to make. (After he calls and registers for the class, he'll move the flyer to his Pending file—more on this later.) He made a note in his planner that he had to decide by a certain date, so he could register in time. Now he can file the flyer without any risk of forgetting, since his planner will remind him, and he'll know where to find it when he needs it.

If you've heard the rule "Handle each piece of paper only once," you'll notice I'm breaking it: That rule usually doesn't work. Tom would have to drop everything as soon as the class brochure arrived in the mail, fill out the registration form, and write the check right then and there. But first he'd have to make the phone call to decide if he wanted to sign up for the class. By the time he'd finished all this, he'd be late for the staff meeting. Clearly, the maxim about handling a piece of paper only once is silly. However, it contains a grain of truth. We tend to handle papers absentmindedly, shuffling them from one pile to another over and over again. This desktop shuffle doesn't work either. The solution is a happy medium— each time you encounter a piece of paper, decide what your next action will be, then file it accordingly in your action files. You can also make a note in your planner as a backup. You'll handle those papers two or three times instead of ten.

We continued to sort Tom's paper into files based on the action he'll take with each one. He added the reminder card from his dentist to his Phone Calls file. Unread magazines and newsletters go in a Reading file. (In Chapter 9, "Surviving Information Overload," I'll discuss what to do if this file is bulging.) Papers to give to other people go into their respective files. Tom made a file labeled Accountant, to hold tax-deductible expenses. He labeled another file for papers to bring to the Staff Meeting (this file also holds the meeting agenda). Bills to be paid go together in a file marked Bills. Since Tom often mails clippings to people, he created a Correspondence file to hold the article for his daughter. Then he made a file for Cities to hold information about places he might want to live. Because Tom loves to buy things for people, he had saved many ads for gifts he might buy. He wanted to make a file for Gifts, but he also buys things for himself, so we created an Errands file, which includes gifts. In this folder we dropped everything from shopping lists to his dry-cleaning ticket. We made a Photocopy file for papers he had to photocopy. The brochures for professional conferences and party invitations went into a file we labeled Upcoming Events. He also created a File category for things to be filed that he didn't want to deal with right now.

Pending File

Sometimes Pending is stage two, after your initial action. After Tom makes the phone call and asks for more information about that class, he'll move the class brochure from the Phone Calls file to the Pending file. He won't put it in Pending now, because he'd forget to call. Only use the Pending file when the ball is out of your court, when you're waiting for someone to get back to you. Before you put anything in here, be clear on what exactly you're waiting for. If the next action is up to you, don't file that paper in Pending. Remember, it's "Pending," not "Procrastination." To be on the safe side, look in your Pending file at least once a day.

In Box

Once you've looked at an item, it should be acted on in some way (filed or set aside for action with a note on your planner), not returned to the In box. The In box is not for long-term storage of tasks you haven't gotten to yet. Your In box is only for items you haven't seen yet.

Continue sorting your paper into your new action files until your desk is clear. If you have piles on the credenza and the floor, apply the same process to them. You don't have to use every category I've suggested, and feel free to add any others that suit you. Just don't create too many narrowly defined categories. Fifteen categories means fifteen folders with only a few papers in each one—that's risky. Better to have eight broad categories; there will be more papers in each folder and you'll use them more often. Every time you open a folder you'll see what else is in there, and this will ease your "out of sight, out of mind" worries. In fact, some people do best with only a very few folders labeled Urgent, Do Later, Read, For Secretary, and a couple more for current projects or major clients. Experiment and find what works for you.

Temporary and Project Files

Whenever you start a new project or plan a trip, everything pertaining to it goes in there. Begin a Trip folder by placing travel brochures in a file folder. When your plane tickets arrive, you drop them in there; later you add the hotel confirmation and a list of things you need to bring with you. Then, when you return from the trip, clean out that file.

Likewise, a project folder stays in your action files only while the project is active. When the project is completed, discard everything except the final draft, the contract, invoices, and important memos, and move the project file to your reference files—don't leave it in your action files. If the project involved reference materials that can be used in the future, don't leave them in the project file where you'll forget them. File them in the appropriate reference category.

Using Color

After you've labeled all your file folders, place each one inside a hanging folder. Color is a helpful visual cue—perhaps red for Urgent, orange for that big Project, blue for Bills to pay. Now place the hanging folders in a file holder designed for desktop use. Office supply stores sell a variety of wire, plastic, cardboard, and metal containers. Any container that holds file folders upright is fine. Avoid the traditional flat stacking trays—they quickly turn into a dumping ground because it's too hard to see what's inside. Stacking trays should be used only for letterhead and your In box. Your action files must be vertical. For even better visibility, get a "stepped" file unit so the folders in the back are visible too.

Don't make the mistake of putting your new action files on the windowsill or credenza. If they're out of arm's reach, it defeats the purpose. They must be kept right on your desk, where you can reach them easily. You may be reluctant to "add more clutter" to your desk, but these action files will *replace* the clutter on your desk if you use them regularly. Or you can put them in the desk drawer closest to you. Soon, using your action files will become second nature. You'll wonder how you managed without them.

Out of Sight Doesn't Mean Out of Mind

Your desktop is now clear. If you're worried that out of sight means out of mind, remember, the action files don't stand alone—they work in tandem with your planner. Tom jotted in his planner the party he planned to attend, the date when his accountant needed his tax records (he also noted a reminder to gather his records the week before), the deadline for that class registration, a note to return his brother's CDs, and the deadline for arrangements for his next trip. (He had plenty of time, but he made up an arbitrary deadline to ensure that he'd act in time to get good deals on airfare and the hotel room.)

Leave time to follow through with things—otherwise your action files will turn into procrastination files. Any big project in your action files deserves work sessions blocked out in your planner. Also, schedule a few hours a week to deal with miscellaneous. Appointments are for you, too, not just for staff meetings and the dentist.

Getting Through the Backlog

Using his planner, Tom mapped out the following steps to work his way through the backlog. The first week he called some friends who had lived in one of the cities he was considering moving to, made the dentist appointment, called to get information about the class, and began to gather tax papers for his accountant. The second week he mailed a check to sign up for the class, paid his bills, delivered the tax papers to his accountant, and mailed the article to his daughter. The third week he went for his dental checkup, made arrangements for his next trip, and started catching up on his professional reading. The fourth week he took care of a disputed health insurance claim, returned the CDs to his brother, and did more professional reading.

You see how Tom paced himself, chipping away at the tasks, week after week. After a couple of months he got caught up. He got into the habit of looking ahead and taking action in advance. For example, handling the disputed health insurance claim didn't have to be done right away, but Tom knew he had more time to do it now than he would later. Now, when the inevitable busy times hit, he no longer panics. There's no need to—things have already been taken care of.

The Sooner You Decide, the Better

What if the tasks in your action files exceed your available time? You may need an extra fifteen hours a week to catch up, but you have only three hours. Now that you see the big picture, you're in a powerful position. You can decide what *not* to do, to free up time for what really counts. Decisiveness is critical. Being unrealistic about what you have time to do only bogs you down and makes it harder to get the most important things done. When you look in your action files, keep your goals and priorities in mind. Any task that doesn't fit (beyond necessities like paying your taxes or fixing your stairs so the building inspector doesn't condemn your house) has got to go. This seems drastic, but you're if you're not going to do something, you may as well face up to it now. This releases you from the guilt and frees your energy for what's most important.

Reality Check

In Tom's case, it was clear that if he wanted to move within the next two years, some activities had to be dropped. He needed to free up a couple hours a week for more patients—he needed to save money for the move. He decided not to attend a professional conference that, in the larger scheme of things, wasn't very important. He resigned from the committee that had been taking too much of his time. He discarded most of the film and lecture schedules he'd normally save—he wouldn't have much time to attend, and keeping so many schedules around would just make him frustrated. He threw out, without opening, the long-distance calling plan offers. He had better things to do than study his phone bill—which wasn't that large anyhow—then do it over again when the inevitable new plans arrive next month. Making these decisions didn't just clear his desk for now. He was primed to discard a lot of the paper that would come his way in the future.

If you have piles of professional or business publications you never have time to read, you have two choices. If career advancement is a major goal, and you simply have no hope of advancement without this reading, schedule several hours a week to catch up. Once you're caught up, schedule a couple hours a week to stay caught up. You may need to *stop* doing something else to free up the necessary time. But first, take a close look at what you think you have to read. Tom looked at his pile of magazines and journals and, realizing he was no longer strongly interested in some of them, decided to donate them to the library. Yes, he'd paid good money for them, but hoarding them unread doesn't give him the money back. Time is the most important thing; it's the only resource we have that is in limited supply.

How about social events? Tom pondered the second party invitation, from someone he was not especially fond of. His planner showed he had no other commitment for that evening. The old, unfocused Tom would have gone to that party. But this time, he decided not to go. Now he's focused on living the life he wants, and there's lots to be done. He wants to move, get settled in his new home, and get his practice up and running again so he can pay his daughter's college tuition. Saying no to low-priority activities is the only way to say yes to the things he really cares about.

Tickler File

The tickler file is a close cousin to the action file. It's an expanding cardboard file with slots labeled 1–31 for days of the month and twelve slots for each month of the year, labeled January to December. The slots you'll use most are 1–31. The monthly slots are used only when that month hasn't arrived

Tickler File from Globe-Weis

yet. On the last day of January, you take all the papers from the February slot and distribute them in slots 1 to 31 (of course, February is a short month). So a paper for March 7 remains in the March file until the end of February.

The tickler file was designed for people who have a lot of time-sensitive follow-up activity, like salespeople. But that's only a tiny part of this tool's potential. Your tickler file is an excellent way to keep track of letters on which you're awaiting a response, phone calls to return on specific future dates, bills to pay (file these several days before the due date), decisions you must make by a certain date (if you're going to a seminar, you must register by a certain date), papers to bring to meetings, a project you'll begin next month, airline and theater tickets, directions to events, greeting cards to be mailed, dry cleaning tickets, things to give to a friend you'll see on a certain day, and so on.

If you don't have enough items to warrant a daily system, use a simpler version: four slots, one for each week in the month. Several times each week, look at what's in that week's slot.

People ask how they'll remember to look in their tickler file every day. You'll train yourself—those times you used to shuffle around your desk looking for things, you'll check your tickler file instead. After a short time of consistent use, you won't be able *not* to look in it—it's that helpful.

Business Cards

There's little benefit in saving business cards in a jumble in your drawer. To be useful, a card must contain notes about where you met the person, what you discussed, and why you'd contact him or her in the future, and the cards should be arranged in an accessible manner. Don't use plastic business card books because it's impossible to keep cards alphabetized. A Rolodex is better. But better still is contact-management software (see Chapter 11, "Taming Technology"). This automatically alphabetizes your entries and provides almost unlimited room for notes on each person. Best of all, it enables you to do searches—you can search for all referrals who were sent by Bob Smith, all the prospects who phoned you in July, all clients in a certain zip code, and so on. Another advantage of using the computer for phone numbers is that you can keep backup copies off-site so if there's a disaster you don't lose all your phone numbers.

If you tend to misplace phone numbers of people you have appointments with, write the phone numbers in your calendar next to the names. This spares you from hunting frantically for them. (Make sure you also put them in your Rolodex or computer; otherwise every time you want to call them in the future you'll have to flip through your appointment book.)

Processing Your Mail

Open mail in the same place every day so it doesn't get strewn everywhere. Have the phone, stapler, highlighter, and waste-basket handy. Throw out the junk mail immediately. Open your bills, throw away the envelope and the inserts, staple the bill and return envelope together with due date on top, then mark the due date with highlighter. Place it in your Bills to Pay folder in your action file, or in your tickler file several days before the due date.

Junk mail and bills are the easy part. Much incoming mail requires us to make a decision, so people leave the paper lying on the desk because they don't know what to do. Even minor decisions, upon closer examination, often require a series of mini-decisions. But you can still *take an action each time you handle a piece of paper.* Here's how it works: If you can't make a final decision now, ask yourself what information you need, identify the steps required to get that information, and make notes in your planner to remind you to take those steps. For example, you receive a memo about the Fat Cat account but you can't respond until you get information from your co-worker, Mike, who is away on vacation until the 16th of the month. There are two ways to handle this: Make a note in your planner to call Mike on the 16th, then file the paper in the Fat Cat file. Or you can put the memo in the 16 slot in your tickler file. Either way, you get the memo off your desk.

Perhaps you get a brochure about a seminar that you'd like to attend, but you need to talk to your spouse about what's on the family's agenda for that day, and you won't know if you can afford the seminar until after you've paid the bills. So there are actually two steps to making a decision about the seminar: talk to your spouse and look at your budget. If you decide to register for the seminar, that's a third step. Make a note in your planner to talk to your spouse this evening; make another note to make the final decision late Thursday after you pay the bills, and make a third note, for Friday, to call and register for the seminar if that's your decision. It may seem like a bother if you've never used this method before, but it only takes a moment and soon becomes automatic. This method is not just for mail—it's a great way to manage any paper that comes your way. Once you get into the habit, your desk will be clutter-free and you'll no longer waste time looking for things.

Bulletin Boards

You'll notice I haven't mentioned bulletin boards, and for good reason. Unless designated for a specific purpose such as photos, inspiring quotes, or bus schedules, it becomes a dumping ground. Things get buried, there's no guarantee you'll see things at the right time, *and* it's distracting and stressful to have all that in front of you. Do not use bulletin boards for anything you must act on. With properly designed action files, you'll have little need for a bulletin board.

Another option for things you refer to repeatedly is clear page protectors or plastic sleeves. These are good for itineraries, telephone numbers, product lists, computer instructions, and more. You can also use plastic sleeves to bundle materials related to a project—notes, newspaper clippings, computer disks. These come three-hole-punched for insertion in a binder.

Catalogs and Junk Mail

I'm a firm believer in mail order. It's a big time-saver and gives us access to a wide range of goods we couldn't easily get any other way. The key, however, is not to let your catalogs get out of hand.

If you flip through a catalog and see an item you want to order, tear out that page and the order form, staple them together, and discard the rest of the catalog. You'll get another catalog next month.

If you don't want to be added to new mailing lists, here's what to do. When you place a mail order, check off the box stating that you don't want that company to provide your name and address to other companies. If you order by phone, do the same. When you receive catalogs you don't want, call their toll-free numbers and ask to be removed from their lists. Or save all the junk mail you get for a few months, then pay the neighborhood kid who does your errands a few extra bucks to make these phone calls for you.

If you want to have your name removed from mailing lists, call the Direct Marketing Association at 212-768-7277 and listen to their taped instructions. Make sure you give them all variants and misspellings of your name that appear on your unwanted mail: Susie Smith, Ms. Susan Smith, Sue Smith, etc. They'll also need the code that appears on the mailing label. Some smaller or local companies don't subscribe to this service, so you must call them individually to be removed from their lists.

To prevent marketers from getting a hold of your name in the future: When you fill out warranty cards after buying a new product, fill in only your name, address, and model number, serial number, and date purchased. Leave their marketing questions (your age, income, how many in your household, and so on) blank.

6

Time Mastery

You can always get more stuff, but you can never get more time.

Time is the only thing of which there's a finite amount. It is truly precious. To use your time effectively, you must know your priorities and what high-impact actions bring the most results. The most important task may be challenging or even unpleasant, but if you complete it, you'll benefit far more than from doing ten lesser things. Resist the temptation to do quick and easy tasks first just so you can cross them off your list.

An entrepreneur who needs to prospect for new business sees his favorite business magazine in today's mail. He needs to phone his accountant about a routine matter and catch up on a little paperwork. Any of these is more appealing than making sales calls. But he knows that his sales cycle is long, so he decides to start prospecting now. After he's lined up some appointments he can read the magazine, call his accountant, and do the paperwork.

The Killer To-Do List

People often say that to-do lists don't work for them. The list is so long that it's demoralizing, and tasks keep getting carried over to the next day and the next week. The solution is to pick what *not* to do. Twice a week, look at your to-do list and cross off four items with the fewest repercussions. You may have heard of the 80-20 rule, also known as Pareto's law. Vilfredo Pareto was a nineteenth-century economist and sociologist who found that a small proportion of any activity produces most of the results. You get 80 percent of the results from 20 percent of your effort, 80 percent of your profits comes from 20 percent of your inventory. You wear 20 percent of your clothes 80 percent of the time, 20 percent of your clients produce 80 percent of the revenue. This is why it's safe to cross off some of the low-priority items on your to-do list.

Organization expert Stephanie Winston suggests, "Ask yourself, must the job be done at all? What would happen if it were cut? Can the job be delegated? As a whole? Parts? To whom? Is the time expenditure—your own and others'—commensurate with the project's importance? If time expenditure seems excessive, can the task be downscaled: simplified, made less exhaustive, less detailed, etc.?"

Some things simply must be done, and you can't delegate any part of them. Yet there's too much going on all at once. Here's how to decide what to do when you have conflicting priorities. If one task has an imminent deadline, and it's very important, it's clear: Do that first. Otherwise, ponder each task in terms of its potential benefit when completed and potential loss if ignored. This is called "opportunity cost." If skipping a task won't have serious consequences, why not instead use that time to start on a high-impact project for the future?

Diagnose Your Disruptions

Start writing down what sidetracks you each day. After a week or two, analyze your record and look for patterns. If the problem is inappropriate demands and interruptions, learn to say, "No, I can't help you with that now. Why not call so and so?" If your staff lacks information they legitimately need, institute regular updates via memo. If crises are caused by a vendor's failure to live up to commitments, find another vendor. Notify clients—in writing—that because of their delay, you may not be able to meet your contractual obligation. If problems are caused by a backlog of undone work, do whatever it takes to catch up—hire temporary help or put in extra hours. If the crises are due to poor planning, pin down the cause. Did you underestimate the time required, on your part or that of others? Did you underestimate the amount or type of talent or supplies needed? Did you leave out crucial steps? Look for a pattern in what causes your crises and correct the root cause, not the symptom. (This is best done with a time log; see below for details.)

The Power of Planning Ahead

Most of what's done in a panic at the last minute could be completed with ease if started early enough. People suffer needlessly by postponing tasks until they're urgent. They contemplate starting their taxes in January, but since there's plenty of time, they do nothing. February and March pass, still no action. By April they can no longer wait, and now it's a panic.

They scramble to obtain forms. Every CPA is booked. Because there is no time to look for receipts, they sacrifice legitimate deductions. And they make mistakes in their haste. What is unpleasant to begin with has become a much worse ordeal due to procrastination.

Why torment yourself? Do things early rather than later. Do the most important thing first in the day or the week. Then no matter what problems arise later, the most important thing got done. If something's due at work, schedule time a few days in advance to prepare. This way, if more time is needed, it's not too late.

Leave a cushion of time in case things go wrong. We know that working up to the last minute before leaving for the airport is not worth the risk of missing the plane, so we leave for the airport early. The same principle can be applied in other areas. Call the pharmacy to have that prescription refilled before you take the last pill. Buy an extra battery for your cell phone before it goes dead. Take your clothes in for dry cleaning before every single suit you own is dirty. Whether it's your office printer, your teeth, or your car, taking care of problems as soon as they begin to surface takes less time and money than waiting until something isn't working.

Appointments Are for You, Too

Make appointments with yourself, for things that are important but not urgent. This reserves a time slot and motivates you. If someone tries to infringe on your private time, say, "Sorry, I'm already booked for that time." It's true, you *are* booked! Make appointments for things like exercising or calling your dear friend who moved to another city. Do the same thing with work projects—make up your own deadlines. You'll get things done early so you can relax.

Use Your Peak Times

Notice your peak functioning time. Do you feel most energetic in the early morning? The late afternoon? Use your planner to block out at least two- to three-hour hunks of peak time for high-priority or concentration-intensive tasks. Make an appointment with yourself and guard this time! Eliminate distractions: Screen calls to avoid interruptions, close your office door. Don't use your peak times for routine matters; handle those when your energy is low. If someone just canceled a two-hour appointment and you're in an energetic mood, don't use that "found" time to catch up on the mail—tackle something that requires two hours of high-energy effort.

When you plan your schedule, estimate realistically how long things will take. If you're preparing a presentation, don't assume you can do it in three hours just because it took that long last time. If this presentation is on a topic you're not familiar with, allow extra time. Don't forget to allow time for additional work a task will generate. For example, cold-calling prospects will lead to requests to mail literature and, you hope, meetings. And always leave a margin of error for unexpected problems.

Be realistic. Make sure your tasks fit into the hours available—don't just keep writing until you've filled every line in your planner. Don't write a three-hour project into a one-hour time slot. If you plan too tightly you'll be tense and frustrated. For a reality check, keep a time log for a couple of weeks. Then, using your completed time log, compare how long tasks actually took to your original estimate. This will tell you if you underestimate how long things take and help you plan more realistically in the future.

Where Is Your Time Really Going?

Our perceptions of where our time goes are distorted. It's human nature. Keep a time log for a week or two. It takes time, but is well worth it. It's the only way to see where your time is going and why. You'll be surprised at what you find.

To keep an accurate time log, don't write down where your time went after the day's over—the human memory is too faulty. Record it as you go along through the day. Also, don't record it every fifteen minutes—you record too many small tasks this way. It's more effective to record it every time you switch focus. That could be in two minutes, five minutes, or an hour. And don't just write what you were doing, also write what for. When you jot down "paperwork," "planning," "phone calls," write down what they pertained to. Also note your observations of what derailed you.

Reality Check

After a week or two, review your time log. Consider the key components of your job and what you're best at. Is it servicing accounts? Generating new business? Strategic planning? Negotiating deals? Troubleshooting? Public relations? Analysis? Now take your time log and highlight the activities that support your key responsibilities. If you have several, you can use different colored highlighters. You may have a rude awakening when you see how little time is being spent on the most important things.

Find out what's in your way. If lower-priority tasks are eating up your time, look for items that you could delegate. Perhaps you do delegate, but delegated work is often done wrong, causing you to scramble to catch up. In this case, your communication with your delegatees needs improvement. If there's simply too much work, perhaps you could subcontract some or hire an intern. If it takes you forever to write a proposal, hire someone to do it for you, or bring in a partner. Look for tasks you could simplify or even drop altogether.

Compare your initial estimates to actual time spent. Did certain things take longer than you expected? Why? Study the interruptions. How could they be prevented? Notice any recurring problems and think about causes. Did you wait until the last minute to start projects? Did you have inadequate information?

Robin, a client of mine who is an award-winning graphic designer with several employees, spent most of his time running the studio, overseeing details of each job, and doing client billing. He had very little time to act as art director and bring in new business, which is what he's best at and would ultimately help his firm to thrive. We decided he would hire an office manager to free up his time to do what only he can do.

You Can Do a Lot in Five Minutes

Much of our time is in small bits. Use it! Read while on the commuter train or waiting in line or at the doctor's office. Don't underestimate what you can accomplish in five minutes while you wait for that conference call to begin.

Use in-between time while away from the office. While waiting for a meeting, you can catch up on paperwork or plan your schedule for next week. If you're out of your office often, equip your briefcase with envelopes, stamps, pens, highliters, stapler, calculator, Post-its, and that trade magazine you can never find time to read. (See Chapter 13, "Travel Tactics," for more ideas.)

Multitasking

Doing more than one thing at a time is fine, as long as it doesn't hinder your effectiveness or offend others. It's fine to read your E-mail while you wait for a document to print. But unless you want to lose a client, don't work on a spreadsheet for one client while in a telephone discussion with another.

Here are safe candidates for multitasking:

- Scan the newspaper or the mail while waiting for your computer to boot up.
- Skim your E-mail and delete what's not essential while you're on hold.
- Listen to your voice mail while downloading a file.
- Read while on the exercise bike.
- Talk to friends on a speakerphone while you're cooking dinner.
- While watching TV you can: do mending, look through mail-order catalogs, clip coupons from flyers, wrap gifts, update your address book, send cards to friends, go through photos and discard the duds. Keep a basket of such tasks by the TV set.

⏱ Effective Tradeoffs

An executive chooses to take the train into his job in the city instead of driving. In the uninterrupted relative quiet of the train, he reads two newspapers and works on his laptop. Formerly, he drove to work, and while he had more flexibility in his time of departure, he had to work three evenings a week to keep up with his work. He's now doing that work on the train. He decided that the minor inconvenience of conforming to the train schedule is worth it. He can spend those evenings with his family without slacking off on his job.

Another type of tradeoff is buying good equipment that costs a little more because it saves you time and money in the long run. If you buy the cheapest laser printer you can find and it jams constantly, taking twice as long to print out documents, making you late for meetings, plus the $100 ink cartridge needs to be replaced once a month, that turns out to be a very expensive printer. A more expensive model would have been more economical. You may be able to find a moderately priced model that does just fine, but don't shop by price alone. Choose intelligently—read product reviews and go onto the Internet and ask questions in computer user groups. Don't waste your time and money by purchasing the cheapest model you can find. You'll pay more in the long run.

Pacing Yourself

Many people jump from one half-finished task to another, or they shuffle papers repeatedly, debating what to do next. I call this the desktop shuffle. If you catch yourself doing it, get a grip. Author and time-management expert Alec Mackenzie says the compulsion for closure is a good thing. People who continually leave things unfinished, jumping from task to task, end up very frustrated and ineffective. If you are interrupted, return to what you were doing as soon as possible—don't go to something else. Fight the tendency to jump back and forth between tasks.

This doesn't mean you can never take a break. But know the difference between useful breaks and inappropriate interruptions, distractions, and puttering. It's fine to take periodic breaks to get up to get your blood moving—go get a cup of coffee, do an errand. It's quite another matter to continually get up and wander around because you're avoiding work or undecided about what to do next. If you need a break from a long task, don't derail yourself by switching to an unrelated project. Instead, make some phone calls related to the project or walk down the hall to retrieve some files.

Control Perfectionism

Most routine work doesn't need to be done perfectly. Doing an adequate job saves time with very little, if any, loss in effectiveness. Think about what's required to get the desired result, and learn to recognize when you've gone far enough. Ninety percent perfect is usually good enough. Ask yourself: Is my effort disproportionate to the value of the task? Will spending more time polishing a routine letter increase its effectiveness? Will other equally important projects be delayed due to the excess time spent on this one? If it's a monthly report, must it really be done monthly? How about bimonthly? Are you being more detailed than is warranted? Is there a simpler way to get adequate results?

Contingency Planning

Most snafus—from small inconveniences to full-blown crises—are caused by lack of planning. You may think you don't have time to plan, but actually you don't have time *not* to plan. Planning and advance preparation enable you to complete things efficiently because you'll have everything you need on hand.

Get into the habit of thinking in advance of everything that might go wrong. By anticipating potential problems and taking steps to prevent them from happening (and to limit the damage done, should they occur) you'll prevent some problems altogether and lessen the effect of the others. This is especially important with project management. You must establish interim checkpoints at key times, when there's still time to take corrective action before it's too late.

"Contingency planning is one of the most powerful, yet overlooked, tools for success in both business and personal life," Alec Mackenzie observes. "How many times do we discover, too late, that a critical deadline cannot be met, no matter how hard we work? The tendency is to blame others. Often, the fault lies in not anticipating the potential problems more realistically or in accepting impossible deadlines."

Whenever you think of something you can use on a project (a book to read, a person to talk to), even if you won't be starting it for three months, jot it down and put it in a file for that project. Then, when the time comes for you to begin, you've got a head start.

Free Up Your Personal Time

Free up your weekends by doing errands during lunch hour and on the way home from work. Mary had been spending her entire Saturday on errands, which made her very unhappy. She now does them all during lunch and on the way home from work and has Saturday free to enjoy herself. This week, Mary wants to go to the florist, gift shop, grocery store, and dry cleaner. She goes to the gift shop on her lunch hour. She could buy flowers near her office, but she decides to wait till grocery-shopping day and get them at the florist at the shopping center. She switches to a different dry cleaner who's on her route home from the office so she can go during the week instead of making a separate trip.

To do several errands all in one trip, shop at stores that are in proximity to each other. If you must shop at out-of-the-way places, stock up so you don't have to return every week. (If the gas station that has the cheapest gas is not on your regular route, when you go there make sure to fill up.)

Buy things in quantities: Buy enough postage stamps to last you several months. When you go to the dry cleaner, take everything at once. When you're at the office supply store don't buy just what you're out of, also buy what you're *almost* out of. Buy greeting cards in bunches—keep a card collection for birthdays, anniversaries, condolences, congratulations, and so on, so you don't have to go to the store to buy just one card.

Call ahead to the doctor, hair salon, and airline to see if they're running on time. Do the same when going to pick up your child at his friend's house to make sure he's ready to leave when you arrive. Then, honk your horn but don't go in. Jimmy's mom won't think you're rude for not coming to the door—Jimmy's mom is just as busy as you are!

Consolidated routines make it easier to get things done because they eliminate the need to continually decide what to do next or when to do something. Balance your checkbook when you pay your monthly bills. Discard low-priority reading material the same evening you take the newspapers out for recycling.

Don't waste your time on minor decisions. In the store, don't spend three minutes deliberating whether to buy blue notepads or yellow. Is this really worth your time? In a restaurant, don't read every single menu item—just scan it quickly. Don't spend five minutes deciding what design your bank checks will have. Just so they don't have little ducks on them, who cares? Everything doesn't have to be perfect.

⏱ Fitting Things In

Make appointments with yourself to make sure you get to the gym. Sometimes you may not make it on the assigned days, but if you don't make appointments, you won't get there at all! Go to the gym during lunch, even if it's for just twenty minutes of aerobics. When you need a break, rather than piddling around, take a walk. It helps you think and gets in a little exercise. Sneak in a little exercise by parking a quarter mile or so away from work, or take the stairs in the parking structure instead of the elevator. If one of your goals is to exercise more and another is to spend more time with your daughter, you could achieve both by hiking or swimming together.

Time Tips for Work

Post Mortems. Much of our work includes steps that are repeated from one project to the next. Doing postmortems will spare you having to reinvent the wheel each time. Upon completing a project, think over what you learned and how you could make it easier the next time. For example, if your Internet searches usually turn up too many hits, then one day you figure out a more effective search strategy, write down what you did! (This is one case where sticking a Post-it on your monitor is a good idea.) If you run training sessions and the materials often arrive at the last minute, analyze why the materials are late. (Are they compiled at the last minute? If so, why? Is your printer unreliable?) Decide what you'll do to prevent a recurrence, make a note of your decision, and file it right in the front of your training file where you can't miss it.

Telephone. Leave your voice mail or answering machine on, then return calls all in a row.

Use a headset or speakerphone so, while chatting with friends or relatives, you can pick up the living room or do dishes. (You can use the speakerphone at the office, too, but be considerate of the guy at the next desk who's trying to concentrate.)

Waiting Time. Keep note cards in your briefcase and use waiting time to send thank-you notes to business associates who've helped you.

Appointments. If someone repeatedly cancels appointments at the last minute, try to avoid dealing with that person. Unless he's very important to you indeed, drop him. If it's a client, ask yourself if your time wouldn't be better spent courting new clients. Even if it's your biggest client, this is still worth considering.

If you meet with people outside your office (at their office or at restaurants), leave if they keep you waiting more than ten minutes. You can't do this with your boss, but you can with everyone else. Or meet them in your office instead of off-site, so if you're kept waiting you aren't so inconvenienced. Better yet, see how many of your meetings can be held on the phone instead of in person.

Quick Reply. Before you type a formal reply, ask yourself if a phone call would be faster. If you must have a record, write your response on the bottom of the original letter, then make a photocopy before you mail it. If a written reply is required, E-mail or fax is faster than a formal letter. But a phone call is fastest of all.

The Mail. Your secretary, if you have one, should process your mail. Not only does it save you time, it also helps your secretary become familiar with your work.

Reminders. If you're afraid you'll forget that 2:00 P.M. phone call, set an alarm in your computer.

Do It Now. Whenever possible, dispatch routine tasks and requests immediately. Anything that'll take two minutes, do it right then.

Prepare. Keep your briefcase open beside your desk, ready to receive any files you need to take with you to work off-site, whether at home in evenings or on an upcoming business trip.

Make Notes. When quitting for the day, jot a few notes about where you left off. This will make it easier to get your momentum back quickly at the next work session.

Take Care of You. If you don't take care of your health, you'll lose far more time in the long run than you'll save in the short run by skimping on eating well or sleeping. Especially when you're pressured at work, schedule leisure activities (aerobics class, night out with your spouse, etc.) just as you would schedule business meetings or doctor appointments.

Post-Vacation Slam. Many people return from vacation and are so overwhelmed with an overflowing in basket and voice mailbox that before long they're stressed out as if they never had a vacation. You can't do everything all at once, so make a list, set priorities, and do the most important tasks first. Some people prefer to return home a day early from a two-week trip so they can get unpacked, do the laundry, and stock the house with groceries.

Time Tactics for Your Personal Life

- Read on the train or bus and while waiting at the post office or the doctor's office.
- Watch as little television as possible.
- Buy extra sheets and towels so laundry doesn't need to be done as often.
- Cluster similar tasks: a bunch of errands, a bunch of letters, a bunch of phone calls.
- Have a place for everything so you don't waste time hunting for things.
- Hire help to clean your house, mow the lawn, wash windows, do household repairs, run errands. Hire the teenager down the street, or check classified ads, shoppers' newsletters, and community bulletin boards.
- Use services to do jobs you hate like window washing and rug shampooing.

- Take advantage of stores' delivery and gift-wrapping services.
- Select an auto repair service that makes house calls.
- Professional organizers can help you organize your belongings or manage a household move. (See National Association of Professional Organizers phone number in the resource list.)
- If you can't afford to hire help and hate to do something yourself, adjust your expectations. You could vacuum less often and choose not to torment yourself about it.
- Exchange services with friends. Your friend wraps gifts beautifully, you love to cook, so at the holidays she wraps for you and you cook for her.
- No time for even your best friends? Make standing appointments.
- Decline unwanted social invitations to make time for the above.
- Phone your friends to wish them happy birthday instead of sending a card.
- Keep a notebook with a page for each person you talk to regularly—your accountant, your decorator, your cousin who's planning the family reunion. Whenever you think of something you need to discuss, add it to your list, then handle the items all at once.
- Avoid stores' busy times and call first to make sure they have what you want. Better yet, ask them to hold it for you so when you arrive you can pay and get out in a flash. Many stores, from sandwich shops to pharmacies, will have your order waiting if you call ahead.

- Even better, shop by phone with a credit card.
- Plan errands by geographic location. Plan your route in a circle rather than crisscrossing back and forth.
- Don't buy things that are time-consuming to maintain, whether clothing or appliances.
- Don't wait until holidays or birthdays to buy gifts. Buy throughout the year whenever you see an appropriate item. No more panicky last-minute shopping trips!
- Save even more time by shopping through mail-order catalogs.
- When you see something you know you'll need more of, buy as much as you have room to store: two reams of printer paper rather than one, a dozen-roll economy pack of toilet paper, etc. (You'll often save money as well as time.) Then, stock up again *before* you run out, not after.
- If you're shopping for a blouse to wear with a particular skirt, wear the skirt on your shopping trip. This eliminates chance of buying a blouse that doesn't go and having to return it to the store later.
- Buy multiples of basic clothing items like dress shirts or sweaters. You'll cut down on shopping time, and you'll never see it at that price again.
- Make standing appointments with the hair salon, massage therapist, etc. Make them, say, on the first Wednesday of each month. (The 5th of each month is confusing because the 5th falls on a different day each month.)
- Each evening, lay out what you'll wear the next day. Place any work you brought home, things to be mailed, or dry cleaning to drop off by the front door.

Beating Procrastination

Procrastination is giving up what you want most for what you want now.

—HAROLD TAYLOR

Why People Procrastinate

Procrastination is not so much a behavior as a *symptom* of something else. To combat it, you need to know *why* you're procrastinating. People procrastinate for many different reasons.

- Fear of success. If you succeed, others will demand more of you, or an insecure spouse or friend may turn on you.
- Fear of failure. One of my clients, a massage therapist, realized that her fear of failure led her to set goals lower than what she really wanted, which made her procrastinate. She's not inspired

86

to go after the goals she's set for herself because they're not heartfelt, and they don't challenge her.

- Loss of interest in your goal. Your interests and priorities have changed.
- Desire to create drama or win attention and sympathy, according to time-management expert Michael LeBoeuf. If you're always in a panic trying to finish things at the last minute, and on only four hours of sleep, you may garner lots of admiration and reassurance from others. Certainly no one will ask you to do something for *them*—they wouldn't dare, when you're already under so much pressure.
- Lack of a deadline. Goals without deadlines are invitations to procrastinate.
- Too many agendas. Overcommitting, trying to do too many things, will make you drag your feet.
- The power of the *status quo*. Some procrastination is just simple inertia: A body at rest tends to remain at rest. This is the easiest kind to cure—all you've got to do is get started.

The Pitfalls of Perfectionism

A common cause of procrastination is perfectionism, which is often caused by a fear of failure, of making a mistake, or of disappointing yourself and others. People with this problem won't start on a task until they're certain they'll do it perfectly. They may be high achievers who fear they won't be able to repeat their past successes. Procrastinating feels safer than giving yourself adequate time and seeing what you truly can do. If you make *sure* you don't have enough time, you've got a handy excuse if you do a poor job. You may prefer to be seen by your co-workers as disorganized, tardy, lazy, anything other than inadequate.

The solution is to give yourself permission to *not* do a perfect job every time. If you're paralyzed by fear of making a mistake, you need to change your attitude toward risk and failure. If you never make a mistake, it does not—contrary to popular belief—prove how competent you are. It merely proves that you're playing it safe and are afraid to take risks. You pay a big price for this, because you don't learn anything new or expand your skills. Playing it safe is a bad choice: It deprives you of new opportunities and lets you wallow in your anticipation of failures, which makes you even more afraid in the future. There's a lot to be said for trying, even if you fail— you learn something that will make the next time easier, and you learn to act despite your fears, which is a valuable skill.

Keeping busy with low-priority tasks is procrastination in disguise. If high-priority tasks are waiting, doing a low-priority task right then is not a good idea. You really need to make that difficult phone call to Ms. Big Client, but suddenly you are seized with the desire to straighten up your desk. Yes, you should straighten up your desk. No, you shouldn't do it now. Your goal is not to cross off the maximum number of tasks on your list. It's better to cross off top-priority, high-impact tasks even if you get only one or two of them done.

Strategies to Fight Procrastination

Now that you have some insights into your motives for procrastinating, here are some strategies that will help. These don't address the psychological aspects, but they do get you moving.

1. Think of all the things you're afraid could go wrong and do whatever you can to prevent or prepare for each of them. For example, you're worried about giving a presentation because you're afraid the audience will ask you tough questions. What are you'll afraid they'll ask? Decide what you'll say if they do ask. Role-play with a friend. Practice, practice, practice, then get to the room early and check that your equipment works.

2. Rather than focusing on your fear, focus instead on the benefits you'll realize once the task is completed. You know that if you do a good job on that presentation it will help your career tremendously. Then consider the price you'd pay by not doing it—reprimands from the boss, missed opportunities.

3. Ask yourself if this dreaded task will go away by itself if you ignore it. Not likely, time-management expert Alan Lakein says. "You *are* going to do this task eventually. The question is not 'Will I do it?' but 'When?' Ask yourself, 'Since I'm going to do it eventually, do I really want to pay the price of delay?' " And let's face it: While you studiously avoid the dreaded task, are you enjoying yourself? Of course not—you're preoccupied with thoughts about how awful the task will be, and all the while beating yourself up for not having done it yet. This goes on for hours or days, and your suffering mounts. You calculate and recalculate how long you can put it off and still finish in the nick of time. By the time you finally do it, you've

suffered one hundred times more than if you'd just done the darn thing and gotten it over with two weeks ago. The unpleasantness of the actual task itself is nothing compared to this long period of anticipatory dread.

In addition, Lakein notes, the task itself may become more complicated or time-consuming by being delayed. A report left until the last minute will be more difficult—you may not have access to all the information you need and may have to disguise the thin points in your information. A tax return left until the last minute will cost you money because you won't have time to find all your receipts, so you'll lose tax deductions.

So you can either do it now and get it over with, or you can postpone it, suffer all the while, and be left with a more difficult task than you had in the first place. Which would you prefer? Once you see how exhilarating it is to get unpleasant tasks over with, you may even find yourself *eagerly* doing the day's most unpleasant task first thing in the morning—you'll feel great for the rest of the day. (Take it from me, a former procrastinator.)

4. Don't wait until you feel totally ready to start—the procrastinator never feels perfectly ready. Don't fall into the trap of doing endless research or endless preparation. This is perfectionism in another disguise.

5. When you're in the act of procrastinating, recognize that it's you who makes the decision. Rather than quickly putting the task "out of sight, out of mind," slow down that moment and look at

what's going on. Realize that you can take control here. Admit that it is you who decided to watch TV instead of doing your work; take responsibility for that decision. You're not helpless, your will was involved, you are in control. Once you recognize this, work on building your willpower. Practice in easy situations first and build up to tougher ones. This *can* be done. I know, because I've done it, and many others have, too.

Tips and Tricks

- Remove distractions. Get that novel you're reading off your computer workstation.
- Put that memo you must respond to smack in the middle of your desk where you can't avoid it. (This works only if your desk isn't covered with paper!)
- Have a report to write? Jot down notes on points to be covered. If you can't do that, get the background information out of the file drawer.
- Want to resume watercolor painting? Get the easel out of the attic and buy some new paints.
- Having trouble making a certain phone call? Call a sympathetic friend first and tell her about it. Then it'll be easier to make the dreaded call.
- Find some aspect of the job that seems bearable. You have a report to write but are more in the mood to talk to people. Do the research part, which requires making phone calls. It'll get you started.

- Promise yourself a reward. Go for an ice cream after you finish the report, or see a movie.
- Set realistic deadlines, then tell a friend you'll have the task done by the date you've set. Now, you have to do the task—you don't want to embarrass yourself in front of your friend. (But the friend can't be *too* sympathetic or you'll manipulate him with excuses.)
- Tackle tough tasks during your most energetic, alert time of day.

Planning: The Cure for Procrastination

Sometimes people procrastinate only because they don't know how to start a big, complex project. The solution is to break it down into smaller pieces. Let's say you have a huge report to write. Think through the steps involved, make notes, then decide what you'll do first, second, and third; map it out in your planner. Perhaps your first step is to gather information. Collect your ideas by jotting them down and putting them into a project folder. (If you don't have a project folder for this, start one now.) Download those articles from the Web. Make those phone calls. Buy that book. Order any needed supplies in advance. Don't wait until the day you have to start writing, then fritter it away with preparations.

Sometimes there are good reasons to wait. Delaying a project because you're too tired or frazzled to concentrate is wise. Delaying because you don't yet have up-to-date information is smart (assuming you've made arrangements and the information is on its way to you). What's the point in doing it now, then having to do most of it over later? Don't do the same work twice.

"Confront issues and problems head-on. If you avoid them, they'll merely compound, and sooner or later you'll have to deal with them anyway," advises professional organizer Stephanie Culp. "Problems are always simpler to handle at the beginning. Deal with people who are problems early on. If your best friend begins to take advantage of you, confront your friend before it becomes a habit. Delayed actions will only prolong the agony and complicate matters."

8

The Perils of Stuff

Things are in the saddle, and ride mankind.

—RALPH WALDO EMERSON

Eight remotes and three TVs, the unattractive tie Aunt Dot gave you for Christmas, high-tech kitchen utensils with missing parts, kitschy souvenirs, your kids' sports equipment, stacks of magazines and newspapers, socks without mates, detritus of long-neglected hobbies, a shoe box of free toiletry samples, outgrown children's clothes, the chair that needs to be glued . . .

As you hack a path from the front door to your bedroom, you're beginning to think there might be something to the "less is more" philosophy. Certainly, the "more" you thought you wanted has become too much. Many people are finding that the more stuff they have, the less they enjoy it. It becomes a burden.

Consider the hidden cost of things you own: insurance, maintenance, storage, cleaning, repairs, lessons. Take into account how many hours of work it takes you to pay for a purchase—divide your salary and figure out what you earn per hour. If you see the price of a restaurant meal in terms of how many hours of your life it costs you, you may not want it so badly. There will be other dinners, but those hours, once spent, are gone forever.

Why More Space Doesn't Help

Most people think that their clutter is caused by inadequate storage space, that having more closets and a variety of bins in the right sizes would solve the problem. It's not hard to see why: When we were children, our parents admonished us to clean up our rooms and put away our toys. Now, as adults, we are surrounded by advertising for storage units billed as "organizers." They come in every size and color, with all kinds of compartments, trays, slots, and drawers. Such products can indeed make things tidier. But I dispute their being called organizers. They are containers, nothing more. *Your brain is the organizer.* You must decide where to put things, what to keep or get rid of, and perhaps most important of all—what to not buy in the first place. The issue is not "Can I afford it? or "Where will I put it?" but rather "Do I want to spend my time and energy on it?"

Contrary to popular belief, having more places to put your stuff won't solve the problem. Having more space only lessens the problem temporarily because you don't feel as hemmed in—but it actually makes it worse in the long run. More space postpones the day of reckoning and creates more problems in the long run. Of all the people I've known who feel hemmed in by their possessions, the ones who suffer the most are those with the biggest homes and offices. As soon as one room is filled, they start filling another room down the hall or upstairs. Eventually they feel like prisoners of their possessions.

The *Real* Cause of Clutter

The *cause* of clutter is almost never a shortage of containers or storage space. In my ten years in business, I've seen only one or two clients whose real problem was lack of space. The true culprit is years of indiscriminate collecting of stuff, much of it stuff that we don't need or even enjoy having. To put it another way, the cause of clutter is indecisiveness. The clearer your priorities, the easier it is to decide what to keep or get rid of.

The best clutter control method is to form the habit of making prompt decisions. This prevents clutter from building up in the first place. Having limited space helps because it forces you to be selective about what you bring into your life and what you keep.

Lest you think I'm unsympathetic, I have a confession to make—I used to be a packrat. The thing that cured me was living for twelve years in a tiny New York City apartment. I stored things in the bathtub—I'd unload them every morning so I could shower. Then I began storing things under a tarpaulin on the fire escape. The landlord said it was a fire hazard, and if the city fined him I'd have to pay. Finally, I had to start throwing things away or pay to rent storage space. I spent about two weeks going through everything I owned and got rid of a small truckload. It was well worth it. I felt much more comfortable in my apartment from then on. That was years ago, and even though I have much more space now, I've never forgotten the lesson of that tiny apartment. Learning to be more selective about what I bring into my life has served me well.

> The best clutter control is to make prompt decisions.

Why Do We Hoard Stuff?

The feeling of needing to keep things has nothing to do with their intrinsic value. You may be reluctant to throw something out because you fear you will need it later, but another person in the same situation will not hesitate to throw it out. The item is the same. The difference is your ability to take a risk.

Packrats often are perfectionists and lack confidence. They refuse to discard junk because they imagine serious consequences if they need it later. They may have trouble letting go of the past, so they save things for nostalgic reasons. Or they live in the future, saving things for use at some future date. According to Sandra Feldman, founder of the self-help organization Messies Anonymous, people with extreme clutter problems—whom she dubs "messies"—accumulate things well beyond what they need. They're motivated by a fear of not having enough to meet their needs, but ironically they end up saving so much that they're imprisoned. People who have lived through really bad times, who grew up in the Depression or are Holocaust survivors—and sometimes their children—often hoard things that other people view as useless.

For people whose parents used to say "Clean up your room!" as a punishment, keeping clutter around represents rebellion and freedom. But while it may provide a temporary feeling of spontaneity, ultimately it creates the opposite feeling. The Messie mind-set, Feldman says, can also be a facet of codependency. These people are rescuers, so they accumulate things—clothes, magazine articles, spare parts, or household items—just in case anyone needs them someday. They feel they should give these things to their friends or grown children rather than discard them, and they end up with a houseful.

For people who feel like they're drowning in stuff, the temporary pain of letting go of some stuff is, in the long run, much less than the pain of continuing to keep everything and feeling imprisoned. There is "an exhilarating feeling of freedom" that comes once you decide to take control and begin throwing things out, Feldman explains.

The Great Purge

A good way to confront all your excess stuff is to move—this forces you to pare down. If you're not going to move soon, then pretend you're moving—go through everything you own as if you had to pack and pay to move it, then see how much you can get rid of. To determine whether a possession is worth keeping, ask yourself these questions:

- When was the last time I used it?
- If broken, is it worth fixing? Am I willing to spend the time and money to fix it?
- How often do I use it? Could I borrow or rent one for the rare occasions I need it?
- Is it a duplicate, obsolete, or outdated and I'm keeping it only out of guilt because it cost so much when I bought it? (Or it was a gift?)

- Does the bother of cleaning it and finding a place to store it outweigh any pleasure I get from having it?
- What's the worst that can happen if I didn't have it?

If you go through all your stuff with these questions in mind, you'll be able to get rid of quite a bit. Confirmed packrats feel uneasy throwing things away, but they are the ones who have the most to gain. After the initial anxiety passes, getting rid of clutter feels great. It does wonders for your morale and makes it easier to focus. Culling your belongings can be downright exhilarating.

But that's not all—the process itself is helpful: You find things you'd lost. You come across symbols of turning points in your life. You rediscover good ideas you'd forgotten about. Old letters from friends and family photos resurface. You gain perspective on where you've been and where you're going, which helps you clarify priorities and goals. Last but not least, it becomes clear that many things you saved "just in case" were never used, which makes it much easier to part with things in the future.

Go Easy on Yourself

Getting organized is a process; it takes time. Your clutter didn't accumulate overnight, and it won't be fixed overnight either. I recommend setting aside a weekend or two (or more if needed). If you find this too overwhelming, break it down into manageable hunks. Start with the hall closet or the junk drawer in the kitchen. You'll start to see the rewards immediately, which will motivate you to keep going.

It's easy to get rid of the obvious junk, but what about things you're afraid to get rid of? Box them up and store them in your basement for a year. Mark your calendar, and after a year has passed, open the box. Did you need any of these things? Most likely you forgot they existed. That's the signal that they've got to go.

For empty nesters who feel burdened by their grown children's expectations that Mom and Dad will store their belongings forever, make a family agreement that each time the kids visit, they take something with them when they leave.

If you find it hard to part with "good" things like clothes in good condition that you no longer wear, have a swap party with friends. You end up with as much stuff as you started with, but at least it's stuff you might use. Better yet, have a yard sale or donate things to charity. If you've accumulated lots of tennis or bowling trophies, donate them to a charitable organization such as the Special Olympics. They can replace the name plate and put your old trophy to good use.

Once you've pared down your stuff, you may still find you need additional storage space. But you'll need far less than you thought. You've gained some perspective on your buying habits. This will help you be more selective in the future. Perhaps you go on shopping sprees when you're feeling blue, then the next day you survey your purchases with dismay. Maybe you have a weakness for buying anything that's on sale. You may buy things as symbolic gestures—you have thirteen diet books and never go on a diet for more than a day. The first step is awareness.

One family made a rule to not buy anything new except the essentials. Rather than impulsively buying things as they came to mind, each family member began to make a list of everything he or she wanted to buy. At the end of each week, everyone reviews the list and eliminates anything he or she doesn't really need. Many families are able to eliminate most items, and often the entire list is scrapped.

🕐 Living with a Packrat

What if you're a neatnik and you live with a packrat? Attempts at reform will probably fail (you already know this), and nagging can make the packrat dig in his or her claws. You can, however, contain the mess. Allow your partner to be a packrat in a defined space, ideally in a room with a door. Common areas that are used by others are clutter-free zones, in fairness to the rest of the family.

9

Surviving Information Overload

We are overwhelmed by information. We're afraid that if we don't keep up, we'll miss something important. So we keep buying more newspapers, magazines, and books than we have time to read, thinking we'll get to them later. We download information from the Web and add it to the pile (or the hard drive). The time we can actually spend reading it scarcely makes a dent. As the piles of unread information grow taller, we feel increasingly frustrated. Getting rid of any of it is out of the question, because it's all good, useful information. Right?

Wrong! It's not useful information—unless you read it. Perhaps there *are* priceless gems in that stack of newspapers that could transform your life. But this is all in the realm of potential. Information has no inherent value. It has value only when you read it. Information cannot be absorbed through osmosis. And much of it needs not only to be read but acted on as well—which takes even more time.

I'm referring to practical, time-sensitive information that pertains to matters like your job, finances, or health, not recreational reading. If you don't have time to read that novel right after you buy it, that's okay—you can savor it later. But if you're stockpiling investment advice or software reviews and a year passes before you get around to reading it, it'll be obsolete by then! So you need to pare down the informational reading to an amount that's manageable, and feel confident that you will be able to track down *new,* up-to-date information when you need it.

Don't Collect Information Instead of Taking Action

There's often a gap between our good intentions and our actions. Buying running shoes and putting them in the closet isn't the same as jogging. It can even be a symbolic action that *replaces* jogging, which in the end does more harm than good. It's the same with collecting magazines, newspapers, or Web downloads. When you keep information but never get around to reading it, you are getting zero benefit. All you're getting is feelings of guilt and frustration from being surrounded by reminders of all the things you're not doing.

You may be saving it for later, thinking you'll dig it out and read it when the need arises. The problem is you won't remember that you have it. If you don't know what you have, you won't think to look for it when the need arises. Take a look in your least-often-used file drawers, or at your oldest magazine piles. You'll find good information in there, I know. The problem is, you didn't *know* what was there. Which means that if you needed it, you would not have thought to look for it. You might even unknowingly go out and buy a duplicate of what you've already got.

Recovering from Information Addiction

Lest you think I don't understand how much you want to read all this stuff or how important it is, I have another confession. I'm a recovering information junkie. What started out as saving a few interesting articles gradually turned into out-of-control clipping and filing of anything and everything that interested me. And because there's very little that doesn't interest me, this took up hours and hours of my time every week. As a writer, I felt I had legitimate reasons to collect almost any type of information. For a while, it felt nice to think that if I ever was bedridden, I would not run out of reading material. But as years passed and I saved more and more magazines, books, and newsletters, I felt increasingly bogged down. Finally it got the point where I felt knots in my stomach when I looked at all the stuff piled around me.

I decided to examine my habits. First, I cleaned out all my files. This gave me valuable perspective on the sort of thing I'd saved and why. There was travel information, health information, computer and software reviews, legal advice I might need sometime, interesting quotes, profiles of interesting people, articles about personal growth, ideas I could use in my business, and much more. (This, mind you, was only the information from external sources—I had still other file drawers full of articles I'd written, my health and tax records, photos, and personal and career memorabilia.) Viewing everything I'd saved over the years brought a rude awakening. Out of this vast collection of information, I'd hardly used any of it! Most of it I'd forgotten I had. Also, a great deal of it was outdated.

Next, I recorded where my time was going, every hour, all day and evening, seven days a week. I did this for two weeks. It was a pain in the neck, but worth it. Then I sifted through all my piles of unfinished projects and neglected hobbies. I had a revelation: The reason I didn't have time to read and finish things was in large part because I was spending hours every week collecting still more information. I would never catch up; in fact I was getting more and more "behind."

I was so frustrated, I was ready for a radical change. So I made a decision: I'd try *not* indulging everything I'm curious about, and I'd pursue fewer interests so I'd actually have time to complete what I started. What a novel idea! I stopped saving software reviews unless I was going to buy the product within the next several weeks. I threw out ads for items and trips I couldn't afford in the foreseeable future. I discarded decorating ideas that were impossible in my current home. I stopped collecting health articles *unless* they applied to a condition that I, or a loved one, *already* had. I stopped clipping gardening ideas because it was abundantly clear by now that I wasn't going to start a garden. And I trashed my articles pertaining to hobbies I hadn't pursued in ten years.

I was on a roll. Next, I went on a bookstore moratorium. What was the point in collecting more information when I didn't use what I already had? For several weeks I'd cross the street to get safely past a bookstore, the way dieters do to avoid the lure of a bakery. For a writer, avoiding bookstores wasn't easy. But the frustration I felt from drowning in information had finally exceeded the exhilaration of adding a new book to my collection.

After going a bit overboard at first, I settled into some reasonable new habits, which I've maintained for many years now. I collect only information that pertains to current projects, the running of my business, specific things I'm committed actually to doing soon (like buying software I really need), subjects I'm passionate about, and pressing health or financial matters. That's all I need to save. I no longer save information I've read just because it's interesting—reading it once is enough. If I need to track something down again, I can do so.

I also look for reasons *not* to read things. When I start to read an article and I see that statistics are misused or the thinking is sloppy, I don't finish reading it. If the writer can't think clearly—this has nothing to do with content—I know I can't trust the information in that article, so I don't waste my time reading it.

I read the newspaper while on public transportation, so the papers don't pile up. I buy only books I'm likely to read within the next few months. Well, okay, I buy a few more than that, but I've come a long way—really I have. I can look around my home and office now without feeling overwhelmed and discouraged.

Be Realistic About Reading

If your information-hoarding habits are out of control, look over your piles of reading material and notice what you haven't read and why. Do you clip articles about healthful eating but never take action to change your eating habits? Joyce used to do this: She clipped reams of articles about how eating too much salt and fat was bad for her. But her eating habits changed not one whit. Then she had an insight: She was collecting this information to assuage her conscience. This way, she could *pretend* she was going to change her eating habits without having to go to the trouble.

Other folks hoard information because they can't resist a sale. They buy discounted books and magazine subscriptions that they wouldn't buy at full price even if they could afford to, then they never get around to reading them. This is like saying your money matters more than your time. It should be the other way around: Your time is more important than money. *If you don't have time to read a book or magazine, a bargain price does not increase its value to you one bit.*

Digging Out from Under

Okay, you're ready now to pare down your own reading backlog. Start by assembling everything in one place. That's right, crawl under the desk and the credenza and pull it out. All of it! Now survey your backlog and ponder how it stacks up against your available reading time. If it looks like you'd need to spend the next six months to make a dent in it, unless you're a professor or researcher and might actually spend the time, you need to get rid of as much as possible.

Go through it piece by piece and see how much of it you can let go of. Books and magazines you acquired years ago in which you've lost interest can be donated to friends, the library, or a charity sale. Be particularly ruthless with the sort of information that becomes obsolete quickly—computer information and much business, financial, and even health information. Get rid of as much as you can stand to. You'll end up with a smaller, manageable amount of things you really want to read, which feels a lot better than a lot of old stuff you feel frustrated just looking at.

Limit the New Stuff

Your next step is to reduce the flow of new information into your life. Don't automatically renew a magazine subscription, unless you love it so much you devour every issue. Better just to buy it occasionally on the newsstand. Cancel subscriptions for the publications you never get around to reading. If a friend offers to loan or give you a book, don't automatically say yes.

Ask yourself how motivated you are to read it. The fact that it wouldn't cost you anything is irrelevant.

For current events, you can stay up-to-date without reading a daily paper. You can listen to the news on the radio while dressing in the morning or during your daily commute.

Avoid keeping magazines intact—the temptation is too great to read the whole thing instead of only what's important. Use the table of contents to locate articles of interest, tear them out, then throw away the magazine. Carry these articles in a folder in your purse or briefcase so you can read in odd moments of time—eating lunch at your desk, on the bus, even on the bicycle at the gym. Then, every month or two, go through your folder and throw away anything you haven't read.

Read Efficiently

Now that you've reduced your reading load, learn to extract the information in the least possible time. (Don't forget, I'm talking about informational reading here, not that new novel.) Learn to skim—most information doesn't merit reading every word. Get in the habit of reading with pen, highlighter, scissors, and stapler close at hand. Marking as you read ensures that when you see the article later, you'll know immediately why you saved it. Clip articles you intend to save *now*—don't set it aside to clip later. While it's fresh in your mind, jot the file category in the margin. This saves filing time. Then check to see if the date and publication name appear on the clipped article. If not, write them in the margin.

Many people can handle their entire reading load with these methods. But if you still can't keep up, schedule a weekly reading session. If necessary, bump something less important from your schedule to make time. Then every couple of months, look at what's still unread and make a decision:

Either schedule extra reading time or discard it. If it's not important enough to you to sacrifice another activity to read it, then clearly it's not that important, so throw it out. Whether you hoard it unread or discard it unread, the result is the same: It doesn't get read. The benefit to you is zero. As "clutterbuster" Jeffrey Mayer says, "There's no difference between having an unread pile on the credenza and an unread pile in the garbage can." There are two advantages to putting it in the wastebasket. You gain some physical breathing room, and being brutally realistic gets you into the habit of making conscious decisions about how you'll spend your time.

These methods will enable you to get the practical information you need efficiently. Now, what to do with all the clippings? In the next chapter, you'll learn how to set up a filing system.

Richard Saul Wurman, author of numerous books about information design and the man who coined the term "information architect" in 1976, urges us to make information clear and accessible. He recommends that you "hold on to what really interests you and make connections from there." Wurman explains, "It's useless to read something you're not interested in, because you won't remember it anyway. Nothing occurs during that experience that helps your insight and understanding. Once you realize this, you'll free yourself from the guilt of not paying attention to most of the news and information that's out there."

10

Effective Filing

If you have Bermuda Triangle files—nothing that goes in is ever seen again—this chapter is for you. Most people view filing as a necessary evil, something you do only when forced to. Contrary to popular belief, filing is not a waste of time. A filing system, set up and maintained effectively, is a tremendous resource.

There are two kinds of files—current and reference. This chapter refers to reference files only. Current papers, such as matters you will act on soon, the agenda for next week's staff meeting, phone calls to return, and notices of events you want to attend, don't belong in your reference files. Put these in your action files (see Chapter 5, "Managing Your Desktop").

How Much Do You Really Need to Save?

There's no way to file effectively without spending some time, so you want to make sure it's time well spent. Your first step, and perhaps your most important step, is to be extremely selective.

This means learning to take some risks. My method requires you to throw away some paper that might be potentially useful. If you keep everything you might need for any remote possible reason, you'd spend all your time filing, which is absurd. Most people's "solution" is to keep papers without filing them. But if you think you can find it later, you're deluding yourself.

Let's look at the risk of throwing away information. If you're determined not to miss any nugget of information, where will it stop? It's not enough to file that health article. There are dozens of other articles published this month on the same subject, not to mention next month. To avoid missing any of this information, you'd need to read a couple of major newspapers every day and all the health magazines, too. Why not? This information could save your life! Now you've got a reading load that will take up at least half of each day. Ridiculous, you say? That's my point. You know you must draw the line somewhere. I suggest that you draw it much sooner. The time it takes to clip and file a piece of information should be weighed against the time it would take to track it down later if you need it. If you're certain you'll need it again, then file it. But in many cases it's better to toss it out. If you need it later you can find a more up-to-date version.

For most people it's not realistic to clean out the backlog and set up current files at the same time. If you start with the backlog you'll get discouraged as new paper continues to come in. So start by setting up files for recent papers. Then as time permits, purge the older files, integrate the keepers into your new file system, and set up new categories as necessary.

🕐 Filing Myths

Myth #1: More space will solve the problem. Reality: It rarely does. More space can even worsen the problem. It makes it too easy to save indiscriminately, which only makes more work for later. If there are papers you really must keep but rarely need to refer to (such as old tax records), store them, out of your prime area, in bankers' boxes. (But don't use these for precious old documents like antique family photos and papers. Despite what the brand name may imply, these are not archival quality because they're not acid-free.)

Myth #2: Getting a scanner to store information in the computer will solve the problem. This is a variation on Myth #1. If finding a place to store the paper were the real issue, scanning would help because it enables you to store the information in less space. But storage is not the issue for most people. The issue is indecisiveness and your attitude toward risk. Until you have a good grasp on what you really need to keep, stay away from scanning. It's not a panacea and can substitute new problems for the old. (If you do decide to get a scanner, see Chapter 11, "Taming Technology.")

People overestimate the value of information. Information in itself has no value. It has value only if you use it. If you can't find, you can't use it, which means the benefit to you is exactly the same as if you'd thrown it away. Zilch! Being able to find it later—the only reason to save it—requires that you file it properly. This takes time. Now we get down to the real issue: How much time does this piece of information deserve? Often, less than you think. Surveys have found that 80 percent of files are never looked at again. Even if you do need the information later, it's likely to be outdated.

Less Is Powerful

Don't simply ask yourself, "Might I ever need to see this paper again?" With that approach, you'll never throw anything away! Ask yourself instead, "Is it worth the time it would take to file every single thing?" (If you knew exactly which papers you'll need in the future, of course, you'd file only those. But you don't know, so if you want to play it safe you're forced to file everything.) The time this would take is far greater than the time it would take to save less and replace the few items you unexpectedly need.

So you see that being selective is extremely important. When in doubt, throw it out. Don't buy that extra file cabinet until after you've purged; you may not need it. Scrutinize each paper with the following questions in mind:

- Do I still need it? ("I *used* to need it" doesn't count.)
- Is it up-to-date?
- Do I have another article (or a book) with the same information?
- Under what circumstances might I need this in the future?
- Will it become obsolete before I'll need it again?
- Is it high quality? Is it from a reliable source?
- Would replacing it be very difficult, and the consequences of not having it, serious?

- Am I legally required to keep it? (for therapists, doctors, lawyers)
- Does it have tax or legal implications?
- Is it a necessary part of a project or client file?
- What's the worst possible thing that could happen if I threw this away?

But What if I Need It Later?

People always ask me, if you discard something you later need, doesn't that prove you should have saved it? Absolutely not. To save everything just in case is totally impractical. (That's like reading several newspapers and magazines every day to make sure you don't miss some health information, as we discussed above.) If you save everything but don't file it, you can't find it if you need it, so you must file it for it to be accessible. But you'll never need most of it (or it'll be outdated by the time you do), so that's a huge waste of your time. If you throw out more and save less, once in a blue moon you might have to track down a duplicate of something you discarded. That's okay—you'll have time to do that because of all the time you saved not clipping and filing. Occasionally having to replace a piece of information takes much less time than maintaining a vast system full of mostly useless information just in case.

Try it—you'll see that nothing irreplaceable will be thrown away. Obviously you won't toss out your birth certificate. Your anxiety will pass, and you'll find it gets easier to hoard less information. As a result, you'll be able to maintain a powerful filing system in much less time, your piles will be gone, you'll feel better, and you'll actually be able to find things when you need them.

The Right File Categories

Your next step is to set up your categories. One reason people hate filing is that they have trouble deciding what goes where, and they worry that they won't be able to find things later. If your categories are set up properly, this won't happen.

Filing is done in two stages: conceptual, which is the act of classifying information into practical, usable categories; and mechanical, which is putting papers into folders. When the conceptual part is done correctly, the physical part is easy, organizing expert Stephanie Winston notes.

The two most common methods—filing by alphabet and filing by source—don't always work. Filing alphabetically puts related items in far-flung locations. That's why it's usually best to file by concept. If you want to keep your children's records together and their names are Anne and Peter, an alphabetical system puts them in different file drawers. The conceptual method keeps them together.

Most people file things according to what they are or where they came from. My ten years of working with clients has proved that this is a recipe for trouble. My method is quite different and may seem odd at first, but it's far more effective. Simply put, *you should file papers according to what you'll use them for, not where they came from or what they are.*

For example, people save piles of newsletters from associations they belong to and file them according to what they are (all newsletters, regardless of source, get filed together) or where they came from (all paper from that association gets filed together). Unless you're an officer in the association, you don't need to save it all anyhow. Saving it *that* way virtually guarantees that you'll get no use out of any of it.

File by Purpose, Not by Source

It's better to tear out any parts of the newsletter you want to keep and throw out the rest. Ask yourself, "Why am I saving this?" and "When would I need to find this again?" If it's an article about retirement planning, tear it out and put it in your financial planning folder. If it's an events calendar, enter any that interest you in your planner now. If the events calendar has directions to an event you'll attend, put it in your action file or tickler file (see Chapter 5, "Managing Your Desktop"). If there's a good article about negotiation, you need a file labeled Negotiation. In short, cut out what you need to keep and file it according to where you'd look when you needed it.

Contrast this with the usual method of putting the newsletter in a file with other newsletters. You'd miss the events, when you want to read about retirement planning you won't remember to look there, and the next time you negotiate a contract, you won't remember where you saw the article. Filing the newsletter in the standard way is completely pointless.

Now, let's fine-tune your categories. If you do a lot of negotiation, you may need a folder just for negotiation. But for most of us, this category is too narrow—a negotiation folder would contain only a couple papers. Better to have more papers in a file that covers a broader area. You'll look in there more often and become familiar with the contents. So a broader category like Communication is better for most people. Articles on conflict resolution, giving a speech, listening skills, and negotiating should all go into your Communication folder. Anything about aspects of communication, regardless of its source or format—a newspaper clipping, an article a friend faxed you, notes from a communication seminar you attended, a videotape title someone recommended, a book review—should all go in this file. This is filing according to purpose or content, not by source. If this seems like too much bother, for many papers it is. That's why you want to discard as much as possible. Don't clip and file everything you read—sometimes reading an article once is enough.

So far I'm assuming that you tear out the articles you want to keep, and most of the time, this is the best way. But there are some publications you don't want to tear apart, such as professional journals. Keep these on a shelf, organized by title, and in chronological order. But before you put them on the shelves, get a looseleaf binder and a supply of clear plastic sleeves. Photocopy the tables of contents from all your journals, arrange the copies by title, then chronologically within each title. Put these into the plastic sleeves and place them all in the binder. You flip through the binder and look for the article you want, note its issue date and page number, then pull only that issue from your shelf. This is far faster than pulling forty back issues off your shelf and pawing through each one. This system works even better if you add your own notes to the tables of contents to flag articles that contain important information not alluded to in the titles.

Project Files

When you complete a project, go through its file and toss anything you don't need—early drafts, memos, fax cover sheets, random ideas and scribbles. You need to save only the contract, invoices, a copy of the completed work, and perhaps a few key memos. If there's information that you could use for another project—a contract you could use as a boilerplate, research with other uses, phone numbers of sources—move it to the appropriate file. If you must have it in both places, make a photocopy.

Business Cards

Some business cards should be filed by topic and not by name. An attorney you don't know well whom you want to contact on your next trip to Chicago should not be on your Rolodex because you won't remember her name. Better to place the business card in your Trip or Chicago folder, which will also include hotel information, plane tickets, your itinerary, and the like. The Rolodex is good only for people whose names you know you won't forget.

An even better solution is to keep people in contact management software on your computer. If you don't remember the attorney's name, you can do a search for "Chicago," and if you need to see the names of all the attorneys you know, you can search for "attorney."

Tax Papers

Tax papers are best kept in an accordion file. Label sections to correspond to categories that you can deduct—business expenses, improvements to your home, etc. Also label sections for W-2's and other forms, as well as sections for brokerage and bank statements. If you have a business, save your old appointment books to back up your receipts in case you're audited. (See Chapter 14, "The Added Challenges of the Home Office.")

Setting Up Your New Files

Now that you understand the concepts, you're ready to set up your new files. Tinkering with existing categories rarely works.

It's better to start over. Set aside a weekend, or longer if your files are extensive. This won't be as painful as you expect. Actually, it's cathartic.

Start by grabbing a wastebasket and dumping your files out on the floor. Look at every piece of paper and discard as much as possible. As you go, you'll find things you'd lost. You'll come across old projects, providing perspective and helping you clarify your goals for the future. You'll unearth great ideas you'd forgotten you had. You'll be amazed at how much you saved that you never needed. Seeing this will make you less inclined to waste time filing such things in the future.

After you've pared down, you're ready to start creating your categories. Use category names that make sense to you and that are easy to remember. If you have piles of brochures and business cards for local stores and service people, you might label a folder Local Resources to hold all of it. (Whatever you do, don't label any folder Articles or Information.)

File folders shouldn't be too fat. If a folder has several dozen papers, it's hard to find things—better to divide it into subcategories. What subcategories you need depends on your work and your interests. If you're an events planner, for example, the file of local resources discussed above would fill an entire drawer. So rather than one folder labeled "Local Resources," an events planner would need a folder for each category: Florists, Caterers, Halls for Rent, Musicians, and so forth.

Put the most recent papers in the front of each folder. Use staples instead of paper clips. (Or use bulldog clips, which are more secure and hold more.) Many papers have been lost because a paper clip grabs unrelated papers, or two paper clips get intertwined and come off. If you have oversize or bulky items related to the papers in the file, place a note in the file: "videotape of Big Company banquet is on top bookshelf."

Group your file folders together first by major areas, then file alphabetically within each area. The events planner also has folders for Banking, Employee Records, Licenses, and Taxes, but, because their purpose is different, she does not intermix these with Florists, Caterers, Halls for Rent, and Musicians. She places Banking, Employee Records, Licenses, and Taxes into one drawer. Into a second drawer go Florists, Caterers, Halls for Rent, and Musicians. This way, when she plans an event, everything she needs is together.

File drawers should have room to get your hands in. If they are crammed full, it only creates another obstacle. Make them easy to use. Your most often used files must be reachable without getting out of your chair. Moving these files nearer to you will save you hours every week. (People are skeptical about this, but try it, you'll see.) Not only will you save time in accessing papers, but you can quickly return papers to where they belong, which saves refiling time later. You save time on both ends.

Indexing Your Files

If the file system will be used by more than one person, you may need an index. It prevents you from filing car records under Car while your spouse files them under Automobile and your teenage daughter under Honda. (Another reason to group files by category, not alphabet, is that if your spouse creates an Automobile file, when he goes to put it away and sees that there's already a Car file, he'll put them together, preventing future confusion.)

If a file index is helpful at home, it's even more useful for businesses with large file systems. Categories that are clear to one person may not be clear to everyone else in an office, and much time is wasted searching for papers that could logically have been filed in more than one place—not to mention hunting for papers that are simply misfiled. What's worse is when people fall behind on filing because they can't decide in which category a file belongs. A file index prevents such problems. An index is also beneficial when you have a large alphabetic file system and most of your drawers are full, forcing you to continually shift files from one drawer to the next to make room to add new files. That's not so bad if you must add a fat new file to the Z drawer, but if that fat new file goes in the A drawer and it's already full, then the contents of *every* file drawer must be shifted to make room.

All these problems are solved by a file index. However, a paper index, maintained maually, is not efficient. The ideal solution is software that automates your file index, such as Taming the Paper Tiger software from Kiplinger.

Filing Supplies

In addition to manila folders, you need hanging folders, which are sturdy file folders with little hooks at each end that slide on runners on the sides of the file drawer (Pendaflex is a well-known brand). There are several benefits to using them. They permit easier file access by preventing the manila folders from slipping down out of view. Also they help you return the manila folder to the correct place in the drawer because the hanging folder, which is labeled to match, never leaves the drawer.

Another plus is that hanging folders make it easy to keep related subcategories together—you can place a couple file folders, if they're not too fat, into one hanging file. If the files are fat, or you have more than three files that go together, use box-bottom hanging files. These are hanging files with depth. They come in 1", 2", and 3" sizes. For example, if you have a manila folder for car maintenance information and another folder for car insurance, you could put these together into one box-bottom file and label it Car. Place the plastic label tabs in the slots on the front of the hanging folder so the folders within aren't blocked from view. Box bottoms cost a little more, but in addition to their organizing function, they save drawer space.

Using Color

There are some people who are convinced that if they can't see where something is, it's as good as gone. They need visual cues to remind them what's where—the long blue box, the small red envelope. People with attention deficit disorder and creative people find visual cues very helpful. Try see-through plastic file boxes with different-colored lids for bulky objects and translucent colored plastic envelopes for papers. Color provides a cue, and the translucent plastic permits you to see what's inside.

Filing is more pleasant for all of us with bright-colored folders. But color coding takes it farther. It's using color to designate areas—administrative files can be yellow, financial records green, client folders blue, and suppliers orange. This speeds up access and reduces the risk of misfiling. But keep it simple! Don't set up such an elaborate color system that you can't file because you ran out of turquoise hanging folders or mauve labels. A less complicated (and less expensive) solution is to use standard green for the hanging folders, then color-code them simply by using colored plastic tabs for the hanging folder and matching colored labels on the manila folder itself. With this method, an incorrectly filed folder is clearly visible, and you get the benefits of using color.

Taming Technology

Technology is a mixed blessing. It has afforded us flexibility unimagined twenty years ago. Personal computers, E-mail, and fax machines make it possible to earn a living from home. People living on opposite coasts can form virtual corporations. Laptops help us get work done on airplanes.

But there are drawbacks, too. They fall into two categories. Some are inevitable: The network goes down, the printer chews paper when you're on deadline. But many are self-inflicted: You buy the wrong product for your needs, or you buy the right product but don't learn to use it. Most people use only a tiny fraction of their software's capacity.

It doesn't help that advertisers tell us that software can make any job easier and understate the time it takes to learn to use it. The ads imply that we can drop our CPA if we buy the latest tax preparation software, and we will become award-winning graphic artists if we buy a graphics package. Sure, you can quickly produce a newsletter with twenty-seven different fonts, but this doesn't make you a graphic artist. Nor does having word-processing software make you a writer. The computer only speeds up processes. If you can't write or design, the computer merely enables you to produce dreck faster. The element of skill is still up to the user.

A big part of my consulting work is prying the wrong software out of the hands of frustrated clients and getting them on the right track. Usually, the software is fine—for somebody else, or for a different purpose. People buy software with no clue as to what it can do. Project management software won't help you plan a project if you don't input that step A must be completed before step B can occur. A chronically underpaid consultant who lacks the confidence to quote a higher price to clients will not increase his income by using time and billing software. These people are disappointed by software, but the software wasn't at fault. It was human failure—they didn't correctly identify the problem they wanted to fix.

The Good News

If you know what you want to accomplish and approach it sensibly, you can do amazing things with computers. Here's a partial list.

- You can retrieve, then "put back," information with just a few mouse clicks. This is not only faster than finding papers in a file but also prevents the clutter that results when you don't have time to put back paper files promptly.
- If you tend to lose paper, putting information into the computer can help. You know it's in a

directory with similar documents, or you can do a word search.

- Keep irreplaceable documents (family genealogy, titles, wills) safe by scanning them, and make duplicate disks to store off-site.

- Professionals such as attorneys who have very long contracts they want to use as a boilerplate can scan them, then use optical character recognition software to turn them into text, which then can be edited with word-processing software. This spares the bother of typing from scratch into your word-processing software.

- You can easily make duplicates of electronic files to store safely off-site. Keep an extra set of disks or tapes in a convenient place (a friend's house or even your gym locker) so you can refresh your backups regularly.

- If you travel often, it's easier to carry files in your laptop than papers in your briefcase. It not only weighs less, but also you don't have to decide which papers to take with you—it's all in your laptop.

- Work groups that collaborate on projects can easily disseminate and share their text files, spreadsheets, etc., over a network instead of faxing or mailing huge paper packages.

- If you have text from a magazine that you want to share with others, you can scan it, then E-mail or fax it (with fax software and a modem) to others. While this is overkill for the casual clipper, for someone on a research team, or in a field such as public relations, it's a lifesaver.

- Business card scanners are good if you collect a lot of business cards at trade shows and plan to do a mass mailing.
- If you often download articles from the Internet, there's no need to print them out on paper. James, an investigative journalist, keeps his downloads filed on his hard drive. When he starts a new article he does a topic search, finds what he needs, and he's got his background info in a snap. Not only does he save paper, he cuts his research time way down.
- Important E-mails don't need to be printed out and filed; they can be electronically stored with other files pertaining to that project.

Technology is a double-edged sword. The very convenience and portability it offers have blurred the dividing line between work time and personal time. The commute to and from work used to be the only time we could be alone and reflect. Now that has been invaded by the cell phone. Thanks to laptops and modems, the weekend—and even the summer vacation—is no longer a work-free zone. Just because you can do something faster doesn't mean you should. Draw the line! Establish some technology-free zones in your life.

To Scan or Not to Scan

Don't be misled by ads for scanners and electronic filing cabinet software. Despite what they imply, for most people scanning is not the solution to all their workload problems. If you have piles of paper you've left out on your desk because the work is not finished, scanning the paper will merely store the information in your computer instead of taking up desk space. It won't actually do the work for you.

Your first step in determining whether scanning is appropriate is to go through all the paper on your desk. Throw away anything no longer needed. What's left should be divided into two piles—paper to be filed, and work you need to finish. Scanning would deal with pile number one. If you're like most people, that takes care of at most 30 percent of what's on your desk. The other 70 percent is on your desk because the work is not completed. Scanning this would not solve your problem at all.

You may want to use scanning to store the 30 percent of your paper that needs to be filed. That's fine as long as you're selective. But in all my years of working with clients, I've found that most of the paper people want to scan they don't need to save in the first place. Scanning is not a panacea. It takes time. The resulting computer files eat up hard drive space, especially if they're stored as images and not text. If you convert the file to text, the optical character recognition (OCR) process is not totally reliable. Last but not least, it *is* possible to lose things in the computer.

This is why—just like with old-fashioned paper filing—the time it takes to scan information should be weighed against the benefits of retrieving it later. Most people refer later to only a tiny fraction of the information they saved, and bear in mind that much information will be obsolete by the time you need to see it again. For this reason, it's better to discard more and save less. (See Chapter 10, "Effective Filing" for a fuller explanation.)

While it has improved, optical character recognition software is not 100 percent accurate. OCR software is confused by flecks in paper, handwritten marginal notes, unusual fonts, standard fonts that are smaller than 12 point, underlining, etc. (OCR errors are easy to spot in text, but with numbers you have to check every character.) Because of the time it takes to do corrections, scanning is most efficient if you have a lot of "clean" papers, such as typewritten documents in large, simple fonts. You have the option of not doing OCR and storing the scanned records as images, but this takes a lot more hard drive space and you can't modify the text. A compromise is to OCR them so you can store them as text but skip the error-checking process, so long as you don't mind storing any errors for posterity.

When Scanning Works

If you are realistic and don't see scanning as a magic wand, then it may be good for you. It certainly saves space and can speed up access to information through electronic searching. Some people swear by it.

Another factor to consider is how much of your information is already in electronic form. If you have tons of E-mail, Internet downloads, and electronic files you created or received from co-workers, and you have very little information on paper, I recommend scanning the paper so you'll have it all together in one place—the computer.

Most people, though, will need both electronic and paper files on the same topics. To make sure you don't lose things, your paper files should parallel your electronic files. Electronic files on related topics should be grouped together, just as in your file drawers, and their file names should match the paper file names. You can also make a note in both the paper file and the computer file that the other location exists.

If you decide to store documents electronically, you'll need a scanner, the hardware that converts information on paper into digital files. You also need a scanning suite, a software program that operates with the scanner and usually includes an "electronic filing cabinet" to manage the files that result. Together these enable you to input and organize your stuff on your computer's hard disk. You can "file" things together from different sources and in different formats, such as spreadsheets, pictures, and text files. The software includes the optical character recognition engine (which converts the file from a graphics file into text), a file manager, and search tools that permit you quickly to locate files you've stored. You can search files by keywords, text strings, or file type.

⏱ The Digital Maze

Technology has given us more places to store things, which means more ways to lose things. In the old days, a message awaiting your reply was either on the message pad or the answering machine. Now, it can be in your voice mail, your cell phone's mailbox, or your E-mail In box. A phone number may be in your paper phonebook, your contact management software, your electronic organizer, or your paper Rolodex. When you want to review a client's file, you have to look in the handwritten notes you made at your last meeting, your E-mail records, the computer files, some paper files, and notes you made in your PDA when you called the client from the road. Before long, you've forgot where all the info is, or even that you have it. The solution is to put things in as few different places as possible, and be consistent. If most records for a particular client are in a paper file, print out related E-mails and put them in the paper file, too.

Scheduling and Contact Management Software

These two types of software overlap because most scheduling programs have at least modest contact management capabilities, and contact management software can schedule appointments. I won't give details about makes and models because it changes so quickly. I will give you an idea of what's possible so you know what to look for.

Contact management software (some popular packages are ACT!, Goldmine, and my favorite, Outlook) is ideal for people who need to stay in touch with clients and prospects, call back on specific dates, and track clients' order history. For example, Sam is trying to get an order from a hot prospect, Mr. Big. Mr. Big had asked him to call again today. How does Sam remember? A reminder popped up in Sam's software. Sam clicks on it, opening Mr. Big's contact record. Sam reads it to see where they left off. That's right, Mr. Big wanted to know pricing and availability of 10,000 of Sam's new product. Sam calls Mr. Big, tells him that the information is now available, and with a few mouse clicks Sam faxes a price list to Mr. Big directly from his computer, which records the date, time, and file name of the price list he faxed. Mr. Big calls Sam back and says he'll make a decision by next Monday and mentions that he has a big golf game coming up, which Sam notes in his software. Sam sets an alarm to remind him to call Mr. Big next Monday. On Monday the alarm pops up, reminding Sam to call Mr. Big for the order and inquire about his golf game. If Sam sent or received an E-mail from Mr. Big, scheduled a meeting, or mailed him a proposal, all of these could have been recorded in Mr. Big's contact record with only a couple of mouse clicks.

Powerful Client Records

If you use contact management software faithfully, you'll be able to see at a glance the history of your dealings with any client—whether you sent your new brochure or what price you quoted last fall. But there's more: If you have a modem, your software can dial a client's number automatically. If you have Caller ID, when a client calls you, your software can pull up the caller's record, displaying the complete contact history, as soon as the client rings your phone.

A contact manager also lets you filter for people in a particular zip code, people you met at a certain networking group, who were referred by a particular client, or anything else you've entered. A reporter could quickly pull up a list of sources in a specific area of expertise. Filtering is also great for marketing intitiatives and mailings.

The software also permits you to create separate phone books, such as one for business contacts and another for personal. You can even create different phone books for your church or Temple group or for clubs you belong to, then you can print a phone and address list for only this group of people.

You need portability? If you don't want to bring a laptop computer, you can print out your calendar and your client's contact history and take it to meetings. (Also see the section on personal digital assistants, later in this chapter.)

Personal Information Managers

Personal information managers (PIMs for short) (Day-Timer, Sidekick, Outlook, EccoPro, and InfoSelect are well-known examples) can do much of what a contact manager can do, but they're less structured and more flexible. Depending on your needs, this can be either a drawback or an advantage. The drawback of personal information managers is that it takes a little longer to enter information. If you want to note that you received a phone call, fax, or E-mail from a client, with a personal information manager you have to type this in. But with a contact manager, you open a pull-down list that includes phone, fax, E-mail, meeting, request for proposal, and more, and you need only click on the appropriate one. The advantage to a personal information manager, however, is that the lack of structure means it's flexible enough to store ideas, project notes, and miscellaneous information that's not linked to either people or dates. A contact manager can't store information that's not linked to a person. But some hybrid packages, such as Outlook, offer the best of both worlds.

In any case, don't buy contact management or personal information management software unless you're prepared to spend some time researching what to buy and then learning to use it. In my consulting work, for every person I see using such software effectively, I probably see four who are getting little benefit and some people wasting more time than they're saving.

Once you explore the program's potential and learn how to use it effectively, you must use it consistently. You must break the habit of writing on paper, except for tasks you will complete by the end of the day that you don't need to keep a record of. This means that the vast majority of your client notes,

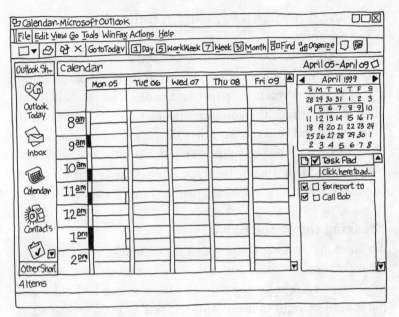

Microsoft Outlook

phone numbers, to-dos, and reminders should be typed directly into your computer. Otherwise you'll get little benefit.

Also, use only one application. If you have your phone numbers in ACT! and your appointments in Day-Timer, you defeat the purpose. It's also unwise to have your business appointments in your desktop computer and your personal appointments in your personal digital assistant (see below). It's far more effective to have everything together—if you have similar information stored in different places, you'll get little if any benefit and cause new problems for yourself. Having too many places to look means you'll forget to look, which means you don't have an overview of your schedule and may schedule yourself to be in two places at once. If you remember to look in all the places, you avoid that problem but create more work for yourself. In either case, you defeat the whole purpose of using the software.

The solution: Do your homework and choose your application carefully. Learn all of its features, then use it consistently. Every time you reach for paper and pencil, ask yourself if you should type it into the computer instead. When you're out of your office and must make notes on paper, upon your return type them into the computer and discard the paper. If the notes are too lengthy for that, type a note in your software stating that there's additional information in your paper files.

Breaking the Paper Habit

To enter information directly into the computer is a big change for most people—but it can be done. To make this possible, you must choose the right software and learn to use it. Your computer must be right in front of you. If you're on the phone a lot, wear a telephone headset so your hands are free to type.

If you get all this cooking together, the payoffs are enormous. You'll have comprehensive records in one place for each client and project. You'll never forget to send a fax or make a follow-up call. When talking to a colleague, you can review notes of what you discussed last time so you know just where to pick up. You will save hours upon hours of time each week that you used to spend looking for, recopying, and refiling paper information. Your ability to use your time effectively will skyrocket.

Another benefit: Using the computer can cure the old "spiral notebook problem." Do you have numerous notebooks, going back many years? It *seemed* like a good idea: You wrote names, phone numbers, reminders, project notes, and ideas, and you could always find things—for a while. But you finish one book and start another, then another. Eventually you have fifteen of them. You can't discard them—there's important information in there. But you don't have time to go through them to find the information you still need—that would be a huge job. So the information in there, good as it may be, is of no use to you. Practically speaking, it may as well be in the trash.

Using the computer instead of paper notebooks or planners will prevent this problem. Information can still be organized chronologically, but you can also locate notes on a person or subject, either by categories you assigned or by a word search. Another advantage: You can make backups on diskettes and store in a safe place, which you can't do with a paper calendar. (We all know someone who lost his notebook and, with it, all his appointments and irreplaceable phone numbers.) Still another advantage to the computer is that you don't need to recopy your phone numbers to your new planner every year—you delete the old ones as you go along.

Keeping Track of Projects

Personal information management software is good for storing information that needs to be accessed from a variety of angles, such as date, task, person involved, or project. The old-fashioned paper method is to keep everything pertaining to the Smith project together in a file, and that includes some matters to discuss with Joe. If you work with Joe on other things too, you might want to put everything you must discuss with Joe together. But if you do that, removing those papers from Smith and other project folders to create a Joe folder, you'll forget to return them to the project folders. Alternatively, you could also start a list for Joe, but that's extra work. Multiply this by co-workers Sue, Bill, and Karen, and you've got a big mess.

Now consider the advantages of using personal information management software. You can review the history of the Smith project at a glance. If you want to see only what's assigned to Joe, a few mouse clicks will show you the list. If you want to see what Joe is responsible for on other projects as well, a few more mouse clicks and there's the overview of everything delegated to Joe. Any meetings scheduled for the Smith account or for Joe are connected to their respective contact histories. They're also linked to any scheduled meetings or deadlines. When you switch between these different views, unlike with paper, you don't move anything. A few mouse clicks enable you to view the information from different angles, depending on what you need at the moment. You don't have to hunt for papers, nor do you have to put them back later. Microsoft Outlook is particularly good for this.

What to do when out of your office? One option is to carry a personal digital assistant or PDA (see below). Another is to print out today's information and everything you'll need for the next several weeks and take it with you. You'll also print out your phone book and keep it in your bag. I've been doing this for years and am convinced it saves me countless hours every week. I don't know how I'd manage without it.

Managing Groups and Projects

Some personal information managers and contact managers described above are also suitable for work groups, meaning that they run on a network and make extensive use of E-mail. But if you want to track things on a larger scale, consider software that's designed specifically for managing teams and large projects

Team management software (such as Team Manager from Microsoft and ManagePro from Avantos Performance Systems) coordinates and tracks team activities. It helps managers plan; they can see at a glance what's on track and what's in trouble. When team members complete a task, they mark it "done," and all the other team members are updated automatically by E-mail. This software consolidates in one place information entered by team members, saving time on status reports. Some applications also have personnel management and employee review functions. This software is designed solely for networked computers and relies on E-mail.

Project management software is designed for massive projects that rely on a complex interplay of people and resources, such as opening a new branch of a company or erecting a building. You enter all components of a project—the big deadline, the interim checkpoints, what needs to be done by whom and in what sequence, how long each step will take, materials and labor costs, etc. You can quickly perform "what if" scenarios to see the consequences of scheduling delays or cost changes. Project management software does for planning what a spreadsheet does for financial projections.

Personal Digital Assistants

Personal digital assistants (PDAs) are handheld electronic devices that run pared-down versions of contact management or personal information management software. An early entry was the Wizard, and more recent models include Zaurus and PalmPilot. Called PDAs, palmtops, handhelds, or electronic organizers, their strength is their small size and portability.

Part of their appeal is due to the fact that people hope to find what Stephen Covey calls "the magic tool." PDAs can be very helpful or very disappointing, depending on the product and the person using it. Despite their being called "organizers,"

I don't believe these devices will, in themselves, organize most people. They are merely electronic receptacles for information—the real organizer is your brain. A PDA is effective only if its built-in software meets your needs, if you enter information religiously so it's always up to date, if it works with your desktop computer, if you back it up in case it's lost or stolen, and if you don't let the battery run down. People who are vigilant about this love their PDAs. Some people have so much fun with their PDAs that, perhaps for the first time in their lives, they have the discipline to keep their phone numbers and appointments and reminders all in one place. If it works for you, that's great.

However, amazing as these little guys are, they have their limitations. Many people, after their initial excitement, end up using them only for phone numbers. In particular, power users accustomed to a serious contact manager like Goldmine, or a personal information manager like ECCO PRO or Outlook, may be disappointed in even the most powerful PDAs. Because their scheduling and contact management software is usually a limited version of the full-featured software in your desktop or laptop computer, power users often find PDAs frustrating.

"Synching"

There's a variety of software available that synchronizes the desktop computer with the PDA via a plug-in cable. Sometimes the software is built in; sometimes it's an extra purchase. In either case, its purpose is to duplicate what's in your big computer on your PDA and back again. But the reality is not that simple. If you "synch" from the powerful desktop computer's software to the handheld device, often not all your data survive the process. The handheld device may run a more limited version of the software or even run something completely different, which means that data can mysteriously disappear.

So before you trust this, spend some time testing. Synch your appointment and phone book files from your desktop computer to your PDA, and then compare the two files very carefully. Look to see if the bells and whistles of the desktop computer's software translate to the little guy. If you've scheduled a recurring appointment such as a weekly staff meeting, make sure that survived the translation as a recurring appointment (you want four meetings a month, not two and not fifty). If you linked a contact record (a person) to an appointment with that person, look to see if it's linked in the PDA, too. If you attached notes to an entry, see if all of the notes were duplicated in the handheld. You may find some of the most important features are lacking in the PDA.

If the results of the above test were not 100 percent reliable but you still want to carry your phone numbers and appointments with you, the best solution is to use your desktop computer for your primary database and use the PDA as a dumb terminal only. That is, synch only from your main computer to the PDA. Don't synch from the PDA to the desktop computer to avoid the risk of overwriting your primary data files with the PDA's abbreviated version. This would be disastrous.

Business Cards

What to do with business cards collected at networking events? Right after you meet the person, jot a note on back about where you met her and what you want to contact her about. If you use a business card scanner, you'll still have to type your handwritten notes into your contact management software, so a business card scanner probably won't save time for just a few business cards. But it does make sense if you often attend trade shows and accumulate hundreds of business cards.

File Names and File Saving

Computer clutter is perilous in a different way from paper clutter, because it's invisible. You can save as much junk in your computer as you want, no problem—until you can't find the final version of that report you slaved over for months because you saved eleven drafts of it under similar names. Precisely because it's so easy to ignore, it's important to be vigilant about how many electronic versions you save and how you name your files. I'm not saying you should save documents less often. On the contrary: Save your work every couple of minutes—don't wait until you're done.

The question is how often you Save As (this creates and stores a second, newly modified version). If too many interim drafts are saved, you end up with a lot to slog through to find the file you need. In a work group it's especially important that files be saved and named systematically. If several employees work on a project and each one saves files with his or her own idiosyncratic names, you'll have a real mess. The solution is for managers to decide—and inform their staff—how many interim versions of a document should be saved for posterity and create a protocol for file names.

With the 255-character-long file names permitted by Windows 95, it's easy to use descriptive file names. In Microsoft Word you can put additional identifiers in the Summary section of each file. But you still must have a consistent method for naming files.

Finally, whenever you finish a project, tidy up, just as you would your paper files. Go into the computer directory, delete early drafts and memos, and change file names if needed for clarity or consistency. Then make your backups and store them in a safe place.

Sending E-Mail

E-mail has pros and cons. Because it's easy and fun, people who are hard to reach by phone or live in another time zone can easily and affordably stay in touch. But because it's easy and fun, people compose messages with little thought (think of all the spelling errors and missing words), and they blurt out things in E-mail that they'd never say to your face. Then there are the tiresome "amusing" or "inspiring" messages that some people feel compelled to broadcast to all three hundred people they know, not to mention spam (the electronic equivalent of junk mail)—both of which waste your time.

Just because you're at the keyboard doesn't necessarily mean you're being productive. It takes longer to type an E-mail message than to say it on the phone, and if you need back-and-forth discussion, E-mail takes days. And with E-mail you're missing a major component of communication—smiley faces and other keyboard emoticons are feeble stand-ins for the vocal cues that enhance a phone conversation. But used correctly, E-mail is a great time-saving tool.

Do use E-mail when you're sending the same message to others in your work group, for non-urgent networking, or to stay in touch with friends in far away places. It's also good when you need to save a record of exactly what was discussed, such as projects or travel information.

Another good use for E-mail is when information faxed or mailed could fall into the wrong hands at the recipient's office.

True, people can snoop into their co-workers' E-mail, but that takes effort. When several people share one fax machine, it's almost impossible not to see other people's incoming faxes.

Don't send an E-mail if the message is urgent, unless you're certain the recipient is in the office and continually checks E-mail. Voice mail will reach most people faster and can be more easily checked from outside the office. If you need a back-and-forth discussion, the telephone is faster than numerous E-mail messages over a period of several days. And it's better to handle touchy situations in a phone call because you can hear the person's tone of voice. Even voice mail messages are better than E-mail for this.

Incoming E-Mail

If you get a lot of E-mail, you don't want to waste time wading through low-priority messages to find a message from your biggest client. One solution is to have two accounts: one for general use, the other—like an unlisted phone—that you give to only your biggest clients. Alternatively, most E-mail software packages let you create filters that automatically route incoming messages from specified people to their own folders.

If you need to respond to an E-mail but can't just now, depending on your software, you can put it in your E-mail program's to-do section, or mark it "hold" so it'll appear every time you download your new E-mail. If you reply to an E-mail message and it's important that you receive a response by Friday, make a note in your planner for Friday.

Much incoming E-mail needs only to be read once. Just like much paper information, after we read it we can toss it. If you need to keep an E-mail for reference, you can create folders for certain clients or projects and save incoming E-mail to the proper folder. But if the E-mail pertains to a project for which most information is on paper, print it out and place it in that file—otherwise you'll forget about it.

Phones and More

Phone technology is changing so fast that I won't discuss the specific features available. Here are some things to bear in mind.

If you spend much time away from your office, a cell phone is a necessity. Not only does it spare you hunting for a pay phone that will accept your phone card, you can also talk and make notes sitting comfortably in a quiet place with related materials handy.

Bear in mind, though, that unauthorized third parties can monitor and tape-record your cell phone calls with scanners and radio receivers. (This is much less likely to happen with a digital cell phone than with analog.) Confidential business news has been overheard by competitors or passed on to news reporters who published it before its intended release, all because someone's "private" cell phone conversation was being listened to. But that's not all—thieves can steal your cell phone number along with the serial number and ID number, which enables them to program other cellular phones to use your account. This is called cloning, explains June Langhoff, author of *The Business Traveler's Survival Guide.* If you're often interrupted or bumped off the line when using your cell phone, you should report it immediately. Otherwise, you won't know what happened until you get a whopping bill. To reduce the risk of having your number cloned, avoid using your cell phone where thieves operate, such as airports and business centers.

If you use a cell phone in your car, put safety first. If you must talk while driving, buy an accessory that will enable you to talk hands-free. One is the Jabra EarSet, a combination speaker/microphone in an earpiece connected to a cord you plug into your cell phone. The microphone, built into the earpiece, muffles background sounds.

Most people don't give their cell phone number freely so they're spared the interruption of low-priority calls when they're in client meetings. But you may need to get calls from specific people. The solution is a device that forwards all calls made to your office to your cell phone yet lets you hear who it is before you pick up. One such product is the M-200 Mobile Phone Companion, which enables you to screen calls just like on your answering machine.

Pagers and Universal Numbers

A pager can receive a signal in urban concrete canyons where your cell phone may not. Carrying a pager also offers an alternative to giving everyone your cell phone number. Alphanumeric pagers display brief text messages, which may spare you the need to make a phone call.

Instead of giving callers a long list of numbers to track you down, a universal phone number (also called a follow-me number) enables callers to reach you anywhere through a single phone number. Your calls can be forwarded to any number, including cell phone, pager, and voice mail.

Variants on this service, like Bell Atlantic's UltraForward, ensure that you're always reachable, but in a different way. You can change the forwarding of your calls to any telephone number from any Touch-Tone phone, nationwide.

The deluxe solution for those who want to be reachable anywhere through a single number and also want some advantages of a personal secretary is an automated personal assistant like Wildfire or Portico. It responds to voice prompts. At your spoken instructions, it automatically dials return calls to people who leave messages, adds callers' numbers to its database, and summarizes your new messages so you can pick which to hear now and which to save for later, and a kind of call-waiting feature interrupts the call you're on by whispering the second caller's name. Since it responds to your spoken words, you don't need to look up phone numbers or dial them. You can assign private mailboxes to your regular callers, which they access through a voice password to retrieve messages you've left for them. Such a service can cost $200 a month, but it can do much of what a human assistant can do, so it's a steal.

If you make a lot of phone calls from your office, a headset is a good investment; it will protect your neck and shoulder from strain and allow you to retrieve and update client files *during* their phone calls, not afterward when it's less efficient.

Stand-Alone Fax Machine Versus Fax Modem

Some people like stand-alone fax machines; others prefer to fax from their computer via modem and fax software. Each method has pros and cons, which is why many people have both.

Having your computer serve as your only fax machine has drawbacks. You can't receive faxes unless your computer is on, and when you're downloading E-mail, people trying to fax you can't get through. You'll need a lot of RAM to be able to send or receive faxes in the background and use other computer applications at the same time. If you need to fax a document that doesn't exist in your computer, you can't, unless you scan it in.

But if you often fax information that exists in your computer, faxing directly from your computer is faster than print-ing it out and slapping it on the fax machine, and the image is clearer. (This applies not just to files you've created but also to Web downloads and E-mail you want to forward to others.) A big advantage of fax software is that broadcast faxing, sending the same fax to a large number of recipients—a laborious job done from a regular fax machine—is quick and easy from your computer. But there's still a lot to be said for having a stand-alone fax machine; and it can also be used as a quick copy machine. I recommend you get both a fax modem and software and a stand-alone fax machine.

Remote Access Software

Remote access software (some major brands are Laplink, pcAnywhere, and pcTelecommute) coupled with a fast modem, enables you, from a distant computer, to dial into your com-pany's network and proceed just as if you were sitting at the main computer. You can update files and synchronize them, check your E-mail, and use any software application you have at your main computer at the office. (See Chapter 14, "The Added Challenges of the Home Office," for more.)

The Corporate Office

This chapter covers matters unique to the corporate office: meetings, delegating, phone and walk-in interruptions, etc. Virtually all of the time-management, planning, desktop management, filing, and technology information in other chapters applies to office workers as well.

You feel overwhelmed, you forget appointments, you frantically search for an important paper, you arrive at meetings unprepared; you stopped keeping a to-do list because it was so long it depressed you; people call to remind you about materials you promised them a week ago. I *know* it's not all your fault. There are a lot of external distractions and roadblocks. Let's look at the culprits one at a time, starting with everyone's favorite: meetings.

Meetings

We all know what's bad about meetings. Let's remind ourselves what's *good* about meetings. You've heard about team spirit and getting people to buy in. But aside from all that, meetings serve some extremely practical functions. They're a chance to address problems before they become crises. They make it possible to share information with several people all at once, which reduces interruptions later.

Some meetings you can't escape. If your boss calls a meeting, you don't have the option of not showing up. But if you have any say, here's what you can do. First, determine if a meeting is really needed. Don't hold regularly scheduled meetings unless there's a good reason. Just because you've always had a staff meeting Tuesday morning doesn't mean you need to now. Do you need a group consensus to get the desired result, or can you solicit input from individuals and then make the decision yourself? If all you're doing is disseminating information, use a memo. Have each project coordinator hand in a memo containing his or her update. Only if there's a problem should you schedule a meeting for the people involved in the problem or the solution.

Plan Ahead

Once you've established a purpose for the meeting, make sure people are prepared. Distribute an agenda in advance. Ask attendees to think of possible solutions ahead of time. This way the meeting time can be spent presenting and evaluating the ideas, not formulating them from scratch. If there are complicated matters to be explained, distribute a briefing memo beforehand so you spend minimal time explaining at the meeting.

Invite the right people. You need those who have enough knowledge of the subject to make valuable contributions, the power to make decisions, the responsibility for implementing decisions, and the authority to represent those affected by those decisions. Some managers feel you need only one person from each department, but this leaves out the lower-level staffers, who are usually closest to the problems and have valuable input. The way around this is for the department representatives to solicit input from the lower-level staffers prior to the meeting. If it's almost impossible to get the right people together, meet by conference call. Schedule a time and distribute an agenda as for a regular meeting.

If you don't detain people needlessly, they won't resent meetings as much. Try to sequence the items on the agenda so people don't have to wait through several topics until theirs comes up; people who need be present for only one item can leave early. For meetings that don't require your presence throughout, bring your assistant, then leave after ten minutes—you can often get the overview that way. Your assistant can stay, take notes, and brief you later.

Timing of a meeting is important. Unless it must be at a certain time (e.g., before the stock market opens), schedule it at 11 A.M. or 4 P.M. This will motivate people to stay focused on the matter at hand and wrap things up quickly.

Start the meeting on time and don't humor latecomers by recapping—that punishes the punctual and rewards the tardy. You can remove all empty chairs from the room when the meeting begins, forcing latecomers to stand. Lock the doors so latecomers can't get in. Some companies fine latecomers, or compel them to clean up the room afterward.

Get Everyone Involved

To encourage participation, require that everyone come prepared with at least one idea for helping the department or the company to function better. You'll not only generate enthusiasm, but you'll get valuable suggestions you would not otherwise get.

If you're the leader, don't express your opinions too early—subordinates may hesitate to speak up. Better to get people involved and get their input first. They'll be more enthusiastic participants. (By the way, if you're making all the decisions, you don't need a meeting—use a memo.)

Your agenda items should be specific. If you use overly broad categories, the discussion will wander all over the map. Set time limits for each agenda item. If the talk digresses to other topics, remind people that there are time limits; interested individuals can discuss further on their own time. Give long-winded speakers a five-minute warning.

But you don't want to be such a strict timekeeper that you discourage people from expressing good ideas. One way is to have the meeting leader and the timekeeper be two different people. The timekeeper acts as police officer and gets people back on track when they run over the allotted time, and the leader encourages participation. Staffers will be more likely to share ideas and concerns if the person leading the meeting is not also the watchdog.

Make Each Meeting Better Than the Last

End the meeting on time. Before you adjourn, review what was decided, make sure everyone knows what he or she is responsible for, and assign deadlines. Then evaluate the meeting itself. Was its purpose accomplished? Was adequate information distributed in advance? Was the agenda followed? Learn from your mistakes and make the next meeting better.

As soon as possible after the meeting, distribute minutes confirming what was decided, what was assigned to whom, and the various deadlines attached. It's amazing how much people forget. Putting it in writing prevents misunderstandings. The tasks and who's responsible for each should be transferred to delegation checklists that are distributed to the parties involved or a project time line that is posted on the wall (or put into the computer, if they're networked).

After you return from a meeting, promptly fill in any gaps in your notes. Then review tasks you've been asked to do and make notes in your planner or to-do list.

Fine-Tune Your Entire Department

Eliminating time wasters is more effective when the effort is departmentwide. People can work individually to correct their own bad habits, but if the culprit is departmental procedures or problems, this is of little use. It's far more effective if everyone—including the manager—keeps a time log for a week. (The boss must participate in this, or others will resent and fear it.) The time log will show patterns like people coming to meetings unprepared, unclear communication, and lost files. Discuss the findings at a department meeting and brainstorm solutions. When a whole department does this, there is ongoing mutual reinforcement and people begin to respect each other's time more. Bob is less likely to be offended if Joe wants to limit socializing so he can work, and Bob will benefit too.

This isn't something you master in a couple weeks; it's an ongoing process. To facilitate this, time management should appear on the agenda for department meetings. Discuss which measures have helped, what hasn't helped, and what you'll implement next. And, as at any other meeting, encourage people to come up with solutions, not just complaints.

Time-management experts Merrill E. and Donna N. Douglass advise, "Choose your [meeting] participants carefully. If you include too many people, or people who don't actually have to be there, you'll have a tougher time getting anything accomplished. . . . Five to eight people is an ideal size for action meetings. Studies show that when group size rises above eight, it is harder to reach decisions. . . . Potential interactions are a function of the number of people attending. . . . With three people, the interaction potential is only 6; with four people, the potential interactions rise to 12; with ten people, the potential interactions jump to 90. The more people attending, the slower the meeting becomes. The sheer volume of interactions between people guarantees it."

Effective Delegation

You may be reluctant to delegate because you can do the task faster and better than anyone else can. So what? That doesn't prove it's the best use of your time. Don't focus on the trees and lose sight of the forest. There are other, more important things that only you can do, and if you don't delegate the small stuff, the things you're paid to do won't get done at all. You literally can't afford to do everything. You want your staff to learn to make decisions so they don't keep coming back to you; this frees up more of your time.

Give challenging assignments to your staff. This requires an initial investment of your time to train and monitor them, and accepting some mistakes—but it's the only way to develop them so they can contribute more in the future. Ultimately, the success of your department depends on this. Moreover, if especially talented employees don't have challenging work, they'll leave.

Delegating is not dumping. It is giving the person the authority—and the elbow room—to do a task. Explain clearly what you expect. If the person doesn't do it the same way you would but the result is the same, let him do it his own way.

Whole-Job Delegating

Whenever possible, delegate whole projects as opposed to subtasks here and there from different projects. The assembly-line approach is bad for at least two reasons. Switching responsibility around among several people increases the errors caused by miscommunication and eats up time. Second, it hurts an employee's motivation and pride in her work if she feels like a cog in the assembly line. Having one employee be responsible for an entire process is better.

Delegating is *not* abdicating. You, as manager, are still accountable for the results of the people who report to you. Tell your staff specifically what you require of them, make it clear which contingencies they can handle themselves and which they must notify you about. Tell them what the desired result is. Say "Let me know if X or Y happens. Unless I hear from you I'll assume it's going okay."

It's up to the manager to clarify an assignment. If your subordinate nods and says "okay," that doesn't necessarily mean he or she fully understands your request. Most employees don't ask many questions for fear of appearing stupid or wasting their boss's time. When in doubt, overclarify.

Don't count on your staff always to remember to complete on time the tasks you've assigned them. Use an assignment or delegation sheet. Record every task, including the date assigned, date due, and person responsible, and if it's a substantial matter, at least two progress report dates when you'll remind them when it's due and learn of any delays you should know about.

Every task needs a deadline or it'll take forever, so set a deadline, even if it's artificial. Rather than imposing your deadline, though, as much as possible ask subordinates to specify their own—you're much more likely to get their buy in. Of course, your subordinate's deadline should be a few days before your own "real' deadline.

Do a Delegation Audit

Keep a log of everything you do for a week, then examine it and look for as many items as possible that you could delegate. Managers often are reluctant to delegate because they fear an employee doesn't have the experience needed to do a task properly. Of course, this is self-perpetuating: The subordinate will never learn to do the task properly if not given the opportunity! The manager must delegate before he or she has total confidence in the subordinate and provide him or her with guidance, tools, and latitude needed to learn to do the task.

Subordinates must feel that they have the authority to handle problems on their own, or they'll keep coming back to their boss. If a manager conveys to her subordinates that she can do delegated tasks faster or better, or she doesn't give them the authority to work through problems on their own, she should not be surprised when her staff keeps throwing delegated work back to her. If this happens repeatedly it defeats the entire purpose of delegating.

When a subordinate turns in inadequate work, resist the temptation to do it over. Instead, hand it back with clear, detailed feedback, so he or she can do it correctly. But let people do things in their own way, so long as the results are acceptable.

Trying to control every aspect of how a job is done is pointless and very hard on staff morale.

> Management consultant Edwin C. Bliss, author of *Getting Things Done*, says, "Giving subordinates the jobs that neither you nor anyone else wants to do isn't delegating, it's dumping. And although it may be necessary at times, it doesn't nourish their egos, encourage them to grow, or enable them to assume the decision-making role that can help to free more of your time. So learn to delegate the challenging and rewarding tasks. The key to delegation is the word *entrust*. When you delegate, you entrust the entire matter to the other person, along with sufficient authority to make necessary decisions. This is quite different from saying, 'Just do what I tell you to do,' which is treating your subordinates as if they were puppets. Nobody has ever figured out how to motivate a puppet!"

For Small Companies Only

A small company or department faces unique challenges. Some employees may be part-time or on flextime, requiring Sue to finish what Bob has started. To ensure that Sue has the information she needs to finish the job efficiently and doesn't have to re-create anything Bob did, create a job ticket to capture information that employees normally keep in their heads or on scribbled notes at their workstations.

In a small company where employees wear many hats, no one feels responsible for anything. The solution is to hold someone responsible. Martha, a part-time receptionist, is charged with being the Order Department. If Thelma, the other part-time receptionist, has to finish placing an order that Martha started, Thelma is responsible to Martha to complete it, or to inform Martha the next day of any problems.

Tracking Delegated Tasks and Projects

Create a delegation sheet with spaces for the name of the task assigned, the person delegated to, date given, date for status check, date due, delays (so subordinates are not blamed for problems beyond their control), date completed, and comments.

To keep track of delegated and pending tasks, create a set of folders labeled with the name of each person you work with regularly: Bob your assistant, Jane your boss, and Henry the marketing director each has his or her own folder. Records of anything you're waiting for from Bob, Jane, or Henry go in that person's folder. Papers you intend to give to these people go in their folders, too. Keep these folders handy in a desktop rack.

However, a big project should have its own folder, and even though it includes tasks delegated to various people, you don't want to remove papers from the main project folder and place them into different folders for each of these people— you'd lose the overview of the project. Instead, leave the papers in the project folder and mark items with eye-catching Post-it flags—each person gets a color. Everything you need to discuss with Jane gets a green flag, so when you meet with Jane, you easily turn to the papers with the green flags even though they're scattered throughout a fat project folder. Assign other colors for other co-workers. You'll cover more in each discussion and won't have to call people back to cover what you forgot. Yet because the papers stay in the project folder, you don't lose anything. (An even better solution is to use the computer. See Chapter 11, "Taming Technology.")

Project Checklist

A project folder should include a sheet for contact information, such as address, phone, cell, and fax numbers for your client, her assistant, and other key people. Tape it inside the back of the folder. Inside the front of the folder, tape an action list for the project. Write all the major steps (use pencil, and leave room for changes) and provide space to jot notes and check off tasks when done. It can include research to be pulled together, people you must speak to, and dates of important letters, faxes, and E-mail sent or received.

Here's the sequence of steps for a fashion designer. First she studies trends, then she meets with the sales force to analyze what did well last season, then she creates sketches, buys sample yardage, prepares garment samples, has a fitting model come in, revises sample garments, has the fitting model in again, prices each style, puts the line together, appears at a trade show, decides which styles to continue or cancel based on orders received, orders yard goods (finding substitutions if necessary), orders zippers and buttons, and works any final bugs out of patterns for production. The fashion designer turns this list of tasks into a checklist, noting deadlines and fixed dates she must work around, such as the trade show. Then she tapes the checklist to the front of the folder and checks off each task as it's completed. With a quick glance she can pace herself to be sure to meet critical checkpoints.

Controlling Interruptions

One of the biggest complaints I hear from clients is that they can't work for more than a few minutes without being interrupted. Either a short project ends up taking all day, or they work in the evening because that's the only time they're not interrupted. An open-door policy is good in theory, but if you have it every hour of every day you won't get anything done. If you go the other extreme and block off interruptions for several hours, a small problem you could have handled could turn into a serious crisis because you couldn't be reached. You need a balance between controlling interruptions and staying informed.

When someone pokes his head in and asks, "Got a minute?" reply, "Not now, unless it's urgent." Then set a time to meet him later—and set an ending time, too. If you've told someone you're available between 4:10 and 4:25, he can't be offended if you walk him to the door at 4:25.

If you choose to speak with him right then, stand to greet him and remain standing—your visitor is unlikely to sit. State how much time you have—odd numbers like "I have eight minutes" are especially effective.

For a drop-in visitor who merits a sit-down meeting, all is not lost. After you've covered what you need to, you can signal "time to go" in a number of ways. When it's your turn to speak, stand up, walk over to her, and edge her toward the door. Or close your appointment book loudly, shuffle some papers, or reach for the phone. Sum up by saying firmly, "In view of what we've discussed, here's what we need to do," then briefly recap. If that doesn't work, say, "That sums it up," "That's it, then!" or "Thank you for coming in." If your visitor still won't budge, glance at your watch, then pick up the phone.

If you have altogether too many casual, drop-in visitors, look at the physical layout of your office. Does it invite interruptions? If you're next to the water cooler or copy machine, you need to add a visual and noise buffer. A strategically placed partition, even a large a file cabinet or potted plant, can shield you. If your desk faces a busy hallway where people congregate, turn your desk at an angle to avoid eye contact with passersby.

If you have a comfortable chair next to your desk, replace it with a hard, uninviting one, or remove the chair altogether. If chairs must stay, keep stuff on them, and don't move the stuff so the visitor can sit down unless he or she has a valid claim on more than a minute of your time—people who can't find a place to sit will not linger. There's a story about a man who sawed an inch off the front two legs of his guest chair. Visitors' calf muscles soon tired of the effort required to keep them from sliding forward off their chair! I don't know if it's true, but it's inspiring. Another option is to meet in the other person's office, so that you can leave when you choose.

You can also control interruptions by establishing closed-door times, say, two hours a day. Put a sign on your door (or on the outside wall of your cubicle, if you don't have a door) that you aren't to be interrupted unless it's an emergency. Use voice mail or your secretary to screen calls at those times. Quiet hours work best when they're department-wide (even company-wide) and at the same time. This makes it easy to respect each other's quiet hours. It's best to do it early in the morning.

What's Causing All Those Interruptions?

Log your interruptions for a week. Note who, when, topic, how long, etc. At the end of the week, study the log and analyze which interruptions were unnecessary, which could have been prevented by better planning or better communication, and which could have been handled by someone other than you.

People often interrupt out of thoughtlessness or a desire to socialize. But to be fair, if you're rarely available, people will interrupt you because they know they must grab you when they can. For people you need to talk to often, schedule regular check-in times for updates and ask them to save up their questions so they can cover several points at once. For example, your assistant could check in with you three times a day instead of twenty. If a person knows he'll talk to you at a certain time, he can hold non-emergency interruptions until then.

You may find the interruptions are partly your own fault. If you don't give your delegatees detailed enough instructions— or the leeway to decide things on their own—don't be surprised that they come back to you. Better to clarify to them when they can use their judgment and what's serious enough to warrant coming back to you. If it's a new hire, or you're awkward at delegating, it will take longer.

Sometimes when people interrupt you it's not their fault but yours. Perhaps you neglected to get back to them when you promised you would. If they need background information about a project or client, put it into a memo and distribute it to all concerned.

The Telephone

The telephone, used properly, saves huge amounts of time. Use it to hold conference calls instead of face-to-face meetings. Call for information instead of writing a letter and then waiting for a reply. A phone call is often faster than E-mail.

Have your assistant handle as many calls as possible. For things that you must handle, have him or her control access to you. Give your assistant a list of people whose calls always to put through and those never to put through.

If you don't have an assistant to screen your calls, it's harder. If you let calls go to voice mail while you work uninterrupted, you may miss that important person who's calling from a pay phone. One solution common in large companies is a form of Caller ID that displays the caller's name so you can choose whose calls to pick up. However, this doesn't always work: The caller may not be at his or her own phone, and an outside number will not display. You can screen your calls with an answering machine, but be warned that this offends some people. One solution is a second line whose number you give out only to people you'll always talk to. Another idea is to trade phone duty with a co-worker. He or she answers your phone for an hour or two, and you return the favor later on.

Stay Focused

Make the most of your time when you're on the phone. Before the call, get clear on what you want to accomplish. Jot a list of points you must cover. Assemble any relevant reports or memos. (When materials need to be reviewed, fax or mail them to the other person and agree to speak at a later date, after she's read and thought about them on her own time.) When you're on the line with a big talker, open with, "I have to leave soon, can we do this in two minutes?" Keep a notebook with a page for each person you talk to regularly where you jot items to be discussed. If you note the person's replies on the same page, your notebook serves double duty: You've got a record of the discussion.

Phone Messages

Voice mail is a powerful tool because you know that the recipient will get your complete message. Leave detailed voice mail messages and have your voice mail announcement ask callers to do the same. Nothing's more annoying than getting a message consisting of only a name and number. (Many people won't even return such calls unless it's someone they know well.) If your caller leaves enough information, often you can handle the query by leaving a message on his voice mail, eliminating phone tag altogether. For example, when you need to set up a meeting, leave a message with two or three suggested time slots and ask him to call back and leave a message confirming one of them.

Message pads make sense for administrative assistants who take messages for several people, but not if you're listening to your voice mail and writing down messages for yourself. If it pertains to a particular project or an important client request, write the phone message on a piece of paper and file in that project file or client file. Once you've jotted down each message, delete it from your voice mail. There's usually no reason to archive old voice messages.

Designated Phone Times

Make your phone calls in bunches, and bunch incoming calls as well. Announce your phone hours, just like doctors do, and have your voice mail (or assistant) ask callers to call again between, say, 2:00 and 4:00. Call people when they're less likely to blabber on—right before lunch, or near the end of the day. One woman found that calling from the airport ("My flight's leaving in five minutes") was so effective that she began telling callers she had to leave in five minutes even if it wasn't true—people got right to the point! Another tactic: If you call from a pay or cell phone, most people understand the need to keep it brief.

Set limits on people who take too much of your time. Set the tone at the start. Don't say, "Hi, nice to hear from you, how are things?" Say instead, "What can I do for you?" or "I have five minutes to discuss the Preston account." If the person starts being long-winded, say, "Give me the short version" or "I can spend another ten minutes on this, so let's make sure we cover the important stuff." Better to say it right away when you can say it in a pleasant manner, rather than waiting until you're frustrated. If you're still having trouble getting off the phone, say, "Let's try to wrap this up" or "I have a meeting in five minutes." If all else fails, say "My boss just walked in—I must go." Another way to deal with long-winded people is to let your assistant deal with them, and if you don't have an assistant, use E-mail or fax.

Try working at home at least one day a week. Make it known that you're available by phone or E-mail if something important comes up. You'll get so much more done without all the interruptions!

🕐 Getting the Reading Done

Here's a unique idea from time management expert Alec Mackenzie: Share the reading load by dividing it up with others in your department; you can brief each other later. Also, a manager can place his or her name last on publication routing slips and ask subordinates or team members to circle items of interest and add notes about what they found relevant and why. By the time the publication gets to the manager, he or she may be able to glean the key ideas just by reading the highlighted sections and the others' comments. This not only saves you time, it also reveals what your co-workers find significant, enabling you to get to know them better. If the publication elicits no comments, consider terminating your subscription.

Using Checklists

Make your own checklists for repetitive and routine tasks. Forms can be used for a variety of things: Preparing for a speaking engagement (your checklist would include things like preparing your visuals and getting your bio to the person who will introduce you), making travel arrangements (plane, hotel, and car reservations, frequent-flyer numbers), seminar planning (rent room, arrange for food, send press releases). Think of all the steps, jot them down, arrange them in sequence, add a box for checking off with some space for notes, then type it up in your computer and print out as needed. Keeping it in your computer makes modifying your checklist easy. (See Chapter 13, "Travel Tactics," for an example of a checklist.)

Using Job Tickets

The job ticket (also called a trafficking list) is helpful for any project involving a series of subtasks performed by different people. (This is different from tracking delegated tasks and projects as described above, which is for a project controlled by one person.) The job ticket is a printed form listing each subtask of a project. As the work is passed back and forth, each person who works on it checks off the subtask completed with his or her initials and the date. The job ticket is stapled to the project folder, which holds all materials pertinent to the job. The status of a job can be seen at a glance.

If You're Drowning

A decade or two ago, managers and executives had their own secretaries. Today, because of downsizing, that secretary is shared by several people, and the managers—those who still have jobs—are doing the work of two managers.

Guard your time, even with your boss. If your boss loads on more work, say that you can't do additional work on top of what has already been given to you—ask him to prioritize for you. If you convey that you're trying to do quality work and meet deadlines, most bosses will respect it. If you're asked to work late on a night when you have theater tickets, offer to come in early the next morning instead of canceling your evening plans.

If you feel anxious about having too much to do, ask yourself: What are you paid to do? Which responsibilities are essential? What are the main things your boss expects you to accomplish? What tasks stands in the way of your focusing on these key objectives? Figure out how you can delegate, streamline, or eliminate what stands in the way.

If your boss keeps loading more and more work on you, keep a list of everything you've been asked to do and show it to him. He may not be aware of how many things are on your plate. Ask the boss which task should take priority. If you're overworked but the department has no money for more staff, consider hiring an intern.

If you're an administrative assistant who supports several people, you're likely to be overwhelmed with work. Arrange for all the people you report to to meet, discuss their expectations of you, set priorities, negotiate, and come to an agreement.

> Surveys have found that executives spend six weeks a year looking for files, phone numbers, and other information that has been misplaced, mislabeled, or misfiled.

🕐 Quick Tips

To expedite replying to business letters, write your reply right on the letter and send it back, keeping a photocopy for yourself if necessary. When you plan to write a formal reply, jot your own notes on the letter when you first read it. This saves time when you write your reply— you don't have to reread it.

If you work with a disorganized person who's always losing files, get a supply of bright red folders. Your colleague will never again lose *your* file; it will be impossible to miss.

To capture things you think of and then forget, keep a small notebook with you at all times to jot them down. If you lose notebooks, write on a napkin or whatever and empty your pocket when you return to your office and transfer notes to the appropriate places.

If your office is noisy in a distracting way, use a white noise machine. Even the motor of a small fan helps.

Travel Tactics

When you take a close look at where your time is going, you'll most likely find travel near the top of your list. Commuting, in particular, eats up a sizable piece of each day. The best way to reduce commuting time is to live closer to work. There are other factors in choosing where to live, but this one deserves serious consideration. Even twenty minutes each way per day adds up to more than three hours a week.

If a daily drive of more than a few minutes is inevitable, use that time effectively. If possible, take a train or bus instead of driving. Besides being better for the environment, public transit enables you to read or use your laptop.

Your Portable Desk

You may already take your planner, briefcase, and cell phone with you everywhere. If you travel by commuter train or bus, you can go farther, converting your briefcase into a portable office so you can do work en route. Buy a briefcase that has the right number and configuration of pockets. Stock it with letterhead, notepads, pens, pencils, highliter, scissors, paper clips, mini-stapler, tape or glue stick, sticky notes, calculator, routing slips, envelopes, mailing labels, and postage stamps. To sort the papers you'll handle en route, you need folders too. Keep two file folders—one for paperwork you've handled, a second one, in a different color, for what you haven't gotten to yet. You can go farther and set up files for Do, Pay, File, Delegate, and Read, which saves you sorting time when you get to the office. Make sure you empty your briefcase regularly.

If you have client files that you often use off-site, rather than keeping them in a file drawer and taking them out every time you go to the client, then replacing them upon your return, keep them in a small portable file box that you can just pick up and go with.

Mini-Office in Your Car

If you drive a lot, you can salvage some of that time. There are accessories such as the Autodesk from Rubbermaid, which turns the passenger seat into a minidesk. There are also adjustable trays that fit over the steering wheel for a work surface, file organizers designed for the passenger seat, and clip-on lights. Order from the Mobile Office Outfitter (call 800-425-3453 for a catalog). Obviously you don't use these while driving—use your head, be safe.

While driving, you can listen to cassette tapes, which are good for things like learning a language or enjoying fiction or bestsellers. But listening to nonfiction, especially business reading, on cassettes has a drawback—you'll want to mark important passages and take notes, which is impossible to do with an audiotape.

Speaking of tapes, I do not recommend using a small

recorder to tape voice memos unless you have an assistant to transcribe them for you. You have enough work already without having to transcribe tapes, too.

Long-Distance Travel

Long-distance travel offers many more opportunities to be productive. For many people, it's an ideal mixture of relaxation and productivity. The change of scenery is stimulating, and you're freed from the constant interruptions of the office.

Think carefully about the best way to reach your destination. Add up the time it takes to get to the airport, get through the security checkpoint, waiting time (at least a half hour), possible flight delays, the actual flight time, the time it takes to retrieve your baggage and rent a car or wait for the shuttle, and the time needed to get to your hotel or meeting location. If all this combined approaches the number of hours it would take to drive from door to door, it may be better to drive (in addition to saving you money). You'll have uninterrupted time to think, and with fewer variables beyond your control, it'll be less stressful. However, if you must read or work on your laptop en route, you should fly, even if the total hours required are the same or longer. If you decide to fly, take a cab or shuttle bus to the airport to increase your productive time. Leaving your car at home will also save you hefty airport parking fees.

Pack Effectively

Keep a master packing list in your computer and print it out when planning a trip. But don't wait until the last minute to pack. For two days before your departure, keep both your suitcase and briefcase open and handy. Whenever you come across something you need to take with you, drop it in right then. Items you must use up until the last minute, such as your planner, will remain on your list, unchecked, so you can't forget them. Put your business card inside your luggage so if it's lost the airline can track you down. (For security reasons, don't use your home address.)

If you travel often, keep a prepacked suitcase ready to go at a moment's notice. It should contain toiletries, underwear, sleepwear, a second pair of eyeglasses, and your portable office supplies. These items should live in your suitcase—never remove any of them, except to replenish the supply.

Call your airline (or visit its Web page) to check regulations for carry-on luggage. Airlines vary in their definition of carry-on luggage. Your airline may count a laptop, briefcase, or wheels as a carry-on piece. If it does, you'll hit your carry-on limit without even counting your suitcase, forcing you to check something you'd planned on keeping with you. First-class and world business class passengers are allowed more carry-on pieces. In any case, the crew has the discretion to restrict passengers to only one carry-on piece if the flight is full. But it still helps to call ahead to learn the regulations.

🕐 Travel Checklist

Destination:
Purpose:
Date leave
Date return:
Airline:

🕐 **Travel Checklist**

Flight #:
Reservation #:
Frequent-flyer #:
Airport:
Carry-on limitations:
Ground transportation:
Car rental:
Hotel:
Address:
Phone:
Reservation #:
Facilities for business travelers:
Surcharges for calls and faxes:
Health club on the premises:
Frequent-flyer miles for hotel:
Itinerary:

Keep a list of projects you can do while traveling. That project that requires several uninterrupted hours—now's your chance! You can also do fun things you can't do at home—rent the movie no one else in your family wants to see, read books.

Handling the Details

Have your travel agent or assistant handle preparations. Draw up a comprehensive checklist that includes your frequent-flyer numbers, hotel requirements (in-room fax machine? A second phone line for your modem?), special dietary needs, and anything else you need. Keep it in the computer and print it out as needed.

No matter how well you plan, things can and do still go

awry—your meeting is changed, you miss a connecting flight. Nurture a relationship with a regular travel agent. You may find cheaper deals on the Web, but the Web can't help you in a bind. The wise traveler always uses the same travel agent and shows gratitude with flowers, small gifts, or a holiday bonus. For the same reason, rely on one or two airlines and hotel chains. While you'll occasionally pass up a cheaper deal, in the long run it's worth it. If you miss a late flight and need a hotel room on short notice, the clerk who sees your frequent-guest points will suddenly find you a room despite the hotel being "full." If you hadn't accumulated points at one hotel chain, you'd be sleeping at the airport.

To avoid delays, plan your trip so you're not flying out at Friday 6 P.M. and returning Sunday evening. Avoid booking the last flight of the day because if you miss it, or it's canceled, you're stuck. If you plan to rent a car, do so in advance. You'll be assured of getting the size and price of car you need and will minimize your wait at the rental counter. Make sure your credit card isn't near its limit; renting a car will temporarily tie up a sum that exceeds the actual rental cost.

Getting Work Done While on the Road

When making a hotel reservation, ask what the room includes. In hotels that cater to business travelers, rooms may have desks with adjustable task lighting, an ergonomic desk chair, outlets for a laptop, a second phone line for your modem, a phone with voice mail for which you provide your own greeting, and even a combo fax/printer/copier. Ask about phone charges (some hotels charge for using your own phone card and even for incomplete calls and toll-free calls) and charges for sending and receiving faxes. There are horror stories of phone surcharges exceeding the cost of the room and incoming faxes billed at $5 per page. If you don't need much in this department, then using the hotel's business center may be cheaper than paying for a room designed for a business traveler—but you won't know unless you ask. Often you can get what you want for a lower cost by staying in certain hotels, joining a frequent-guest program, or reserving a more expensive room that saves you money in the long run because local calls and a specified number of outgoing faxes are free.

Plan Ahead

Call to confirm all appointments before you leave, so if there are schedule changes you can make the most of your time. Prepare an itinerary that includes dates, hotel addresses and phone numbers, and airline names and flight numbers. Leave copies with your assistant and your family.

Bring notes on people you plan to see. In addition to project or client files on paper, don't forget notes in your computer, such as contact histories in your contact manager. If you're not taking a laptop, print out key contact histories to bring with you.

Make a list of things to do when you return. This enables you to hit the ground running when you get back. Last thing before you leave, call your airline to confirm that the flight hasn't been changed or canceled. Then change your voice mail message to let callers know you'll be out of your office and state whether you'll be checking messages regularly. Otherwise, tell callers how to reach your assistant.

Save time at the airport (and eliminate risk of loss or theft) by packing so you don't need to check your luggage. Make it all fit into a carry-on bag. In particular, money, credit cards, traveler's checks, health insurance card, prescription medication, passport, and eyeglasses or contact lenses should never be in checked baggage. Always put your airline ticket and itinerary in the same pocket of your briefcase or purse; don't use this section for other papers.

For longer trips, your briefcase should contain everything listed above for local travel, plus pre-addressed envelopes to mail things back to the office. In addition to a pager and/or a cell phone, you may want a universal or follow-me phone number if you must be easily reachable. For the ultimate in time-saving phone technology, consider an automated personal assistant such as Wildfire (see Chapter 11, "Taming Technology").

Laptops and E-Mail

If you bring a laptop computer, make sure your battery is fully charged before you leave. For longer (or work-intensive) trips, consider bringing a backup battery; if it's too heavy (or expensive) to carry a second battery, bring an adapter and/or a charger. If you need to dial into your main computer at home or the office, you'll need remote access software (see Chapter 11). For files that aren't on the network, duplicating them on your laptop isn't enough. Bring a backup set of floppies and pack them separately from your laptop so if it's stolen you still have your files. You can rent a computer.

However, if your only need for a laptop is occasionally to check your E-mail, you don't have to lug it with you. Many E-mail providers allow you to access messages free from any Internet-connected computer, which means you can get and send E-mail at the airport, a cybercafé, your hotel, or a client's office. You'll be spared lugging your laptop and you'll avoid paying long-distance charges to access your regular E-mail server.

Use All Your Time

Frequent travelers should join the airline clubs. These lounges are more than just a place to sit and relax. An increasing number now provide desks with electrical outlets (so you can spare your laptop's battery for a while), as well as fax and photocopy machines. Some even offer meeting rooms which you can book, sometimes for a fee.

If you really want to get lots done, don't use only on-flight time, use the bits of time in between, too. Time-management expert Robert Moskowitz suggests that, as soon as you sit down at the gate, open your bag and start working. Work right up until your row is called for boarding. As soon as you get seated on the plane, resume working. When you land at your destination, unless you're in first class, it's silly to stand up as soon as the crew opens the door. It'll be ten minutes before you can disembark, so keep working until it's time to walk off.

Handle It Now!

At your hotel room, set up an office. You can make and respond to phone calls, send and receive faxes, dictate letters and mail the tapes to your assistant, and more. This way there won't be a mountain of work waiting when you return. Jot reminder notes on papers that need attention later (saves rereading them), and if it's time-sensitive, make a note in your planner. Then put papers into file folders labeled to mirror what you have in your office: Do, Call, Discuss, File, and Read. People you delegate to or talk to regularly should get their own files, just like at the office. Then it's already sorted on your return.

Keep an envelope just for receipts. At the end of each day, go through it and make notes on any receipts that are not self-explanatory; then put them back in the envelope.

This will save you lots of time when you turn in your expenses later.

Jot notes on the backs of business cards you collect: where you met the person, what you discussed, and why you'd contact him or her in the future. At the end of a day of client meetings or visiting trade show exhibits, look through all the sales literature, cards, and stuff you've collected. Unless you have a specific reason to keep it, throw it away now. If you must keep vast quantities of what you've collected, lighten your briefcase by mailing a few fat envelopes back to your office.

A Great Time to Read

Bring a folder full of clipped articles you've been meaning to read. During moments that are normally wasted, such as waiting to board your flight, you can read a couple of articles, then (unless you absolutely must keep them) toss them in the trash can before you board. If you do this throughout your trip, you'll return with a lighter briefcase and a great feeling of accomplishment! Of course you can bring books, too. Beware of bringing intact magazines—the temptation is too great to leaf through the whole thing. (See Chapter 9, "Surviving Information Overload.")

The Added Challenges of
the Home Office

Who could have predicted twenty years ago that millions of Americans today would be working from a home office? Some people have jobs that permit them to work from home a couple of days a week; this is called telecommuting. Others have their own businesses that they run from home.

The home office offers many advantages. Even if you still work for one employer, you're relatively free—free of office distractions and annoying co-workers—enabling you to get more work done. Your commute is the time it takes to walk into your study. You enjoy a more flexible schedule and more time to spend with your family, and—last but not least—business clothes are not required. For entrepreneurs, you have all of these advantages *plus* the appeal of running your own show and perhaps making a fortune.

Most of the advice in this book applies to the home office worker, too. But working out of a home office presents its own unique pitfalls. This chapter will help you navigate them.

⏰ Telecommuting or Self-Employment?

Telecommuters work full-time for one employer, and they receive benefits. They receive regular paychecks with taxes withheld; their employer files W-2s with the IRS and pays half of their social security tax. In contrast, self-employed people are independent contractors. They may have employees or be a one-person operation, but they have this in common: They must generate business, they buy their own supplies and equipment, and they provide their own health, retirement, and disability insurance. They have clients (as opposed to one boss) who file 1099s with the IRS (not W-2s). All taxes are their responsibility, including their entire social security tax, because they are both employee and employer. They can deduct substantial business expenses, possibly including their home office.

Although you won't have interruptions from irritating co-workers, you may have interruptions from neighbors, children, and a spouse who may not understand that you're working. You won't have to fight the morning traffic, but you may have trouble getting out of bed—who will notice if you sleep till 9:00? You finally get up and your morning jog too easily becomes a leisurely stroll through the park. Finally you buckle down to work, but then you get up to water the plants, and next thing you know, you're watching a soap opera. If your son is sick, your spouse may assume you'll deal with it because you're already home. Your computer is misbehaving and there's no techno-whiz down the hall to fix it. Your neighbor drops by to socialize, and suddenly the day is over.

Ahh, It's So Quiet . . . It's Getting to Me!

Even if you are quite disciplined and have none of these problems, it's not easy to work, day after day, in a quiet room with few or no interruptions. Turning the radio on isn't the same as hearing the buzz of co-workers in the background. After a few days of being thrilled at how much you are getting done, you begin to go batty. Even if you disliked your co-workers, you may find you prefer some social stimulation to none at all.

The same thing that makes working at home seem appealing is what makes it difficult. All our lives we've been expected to get up, get dressed, arrive at a certain time, sit at our desk, and perform work dictated to us by fellow employees and bosses. We toil away, surrounded by others who are working on related tasks, eat lunch at a predictable time, then leave at an appointed hour. Much as we may have chafed at it, we had a structure to work in and around. When you work at home, it's completely different.

You may find, to your surprise, that you need the ritual of putting on a suit and arriving at 9:00, surrounded by people similarly dressed, and that you need the buzz of people working around you. You don't know how much you need this until it's taken away. Left to yourself, you may have no discipline at all.

If you're in business for yourself, you also face the challenges of bringing in business, keeping clients happy, making sure you get paid, and remembering to not run out of laser toner. Deciding what to do each day is no longer a simple time-management decision—it's a strategy decision. You must constantly plan, evaluate, and make decisions, with no co-workers to bounce ideas off of.

What It Takes

Working at home isn't for everyone. People who are most likely to succeed are self-starters, goal-oriented individuals who can create their own structure and follow it and are disciplined enough to work independently. Those who need an external structure and a boss around to prod them into action won't do well in a home office. People who greatly enjoy the camaraderie of the workplace will probably be miserable. In addition, to work at home you need a supportive family and child care arrangements. You have to like your work—very few people who work only for the money, keeping one eye on the clock, will have the discipline required. However, with the right ingredients, planning, and practice, you can make it work.

The Right Office Space and Equipment

You need a dedicated area where you can leave your work out (not the dining room table), and if you have kids, you must have a door to shut. You'll need a phone, a computer, a fax machine, and a printer. As in the corporate office, the ideal desk is L-shaped or U-shaped. You need at least one file drawer that you can reach without leaving your desk.

An adjustable chair with good lower-back support is essential, along with a wrist pad for your keyboard and perhaps an adjustable stool for your feet. One advantage of working at home is that you can choose a good chair with back support and lighting that's good for your eyes. Better to have several lamps rather than one bright overhead light. Don't place your monitor so light reflects off the screen. Your office should be reasonably quiet but not too quiet. Play upbeat music on the radio or stereo, but have the remote close at hand so you can quickly turn down the volume when the phone rings.

Phones and Faxes

Consider quality, not just price. Poor sound quality will not impress your clients. Get a second line for your fax machine or fax modem. You may think you can't afford a second line, but the truth is that you can't afford not to have one. Giving callers a busy signal when you're faxing or downloading your E-mail wastes their time and makes you appear unprofessional. Even worse is when someone is trying to fax you and you answer the phone, especially if it happens repeatedly. This screams "amateur." If you can't afford a second line, at least get equipment that can distinguish an incoming fax from a phone call.

Even a small business can benefit from a voice mail system that allows callers to press 1 for your address and fax number, press 2 for your hours of operation, press 3 to place an order, or press 4 to speak to someone. Three-way calling is helpful for conference calls. If you spend a lot of time on the phone, invest in a telephone headset. It is not only easier on your neck and shoulder, but you can walk around while talking, which helps keep your energy up.

While some people hate call waiting, it has a major advantage. It's the next best thing to a secretary—it permits important calls to reach you promptly. Without it, you don't know who's calling until you check your voice mail, and even a minute later can be too late. You race to call the person back, he's already left, and you now have a five-round game of phone tag. Many people feel that the advantage of being available to callers far outweighs the brief interruption of the second call coming in. When it does, switch to that line only long enough to find out who the second caller is, say you'll call back, then quickly get back to the first caller. If the first caller complains about this brief interruption, point out that he, too, benefits from being able to reach you if it's urgent. Most callers are reasonable.

If you want to screen phone calls while you work, use an answering machine, or better yet, Caller I.D.—it's more professional.

Other Equipment and Supplies

If you're making several runs to the copy shop each week or, worse, delaying sending information to prospects because you couldn't get to the copy shop, consider buying a copier. For quick convenience copies, you can use your fax machine, but you can't do this for bound material, and you probably wouldn't want to send these to a prospect. (For information on fax machines, see Chapter 11, "Taming Technology.")

Don't let yourself run out of supplies. If you're accustomed to working in a corporate office, this will take some getting used to. You don't want to find out that you're out of laser toner thirty minutes before that proposal is due! Buy in bulk.

Making Your Own Schedule

Most of us have arranged our personal lives around the nine-to-five job and therefore have no choice but to do personal and family things in the evenings or on the weekends, or use up one of our personal days. One of the main joys of working from home is that you are free to set up a more flexible schedule that suits you. One of the biggest perils of working at home is that you are free to set up a more flexible schedule that suits you.

When you work at home, your schedule can be tailored to suit you, but you still need some kind of structure. You might get up at 6:00 to exercise, make long-distance calls before the rates go up at 8:00, meet with clients in the morning because that's when you're sharpest, then make phone calls and write proposals in the afternoon. Your schedule may be structured around a major interest or commitment: If your child finishes school at 3:00 you can visit clients in the early or midafternoon so you can pick your child up on the return trip. You can work nontraditional hours—do some work early in the morning when the family's still asleep, or late in the evening after the kids are asleep. If making your business a success is the most important thing and you have no children or a supportive spouse, you can work in the evening whenever you feel like it. If your greatest joy is sailboat racing and you want to take long weekends in the summer, you'll do whatever is necessary to ensure that your work is done by Thursday evening. All of these are types of structure. You need structure or you won't get much done and your clients won't know when to reach you.

A weekly checklist can be helpful. Include actions to grow your business in addition to routine administrative and house-keeping tasks. Your weekly checklist might include: one networking lunch, five networking phone calls, two hours spent reading trade periodicals, ten calls to prospective new clients, three calls to past clients, reminders to put out the recycling on Wednesday, filing, check for which office supplies are running low, pay the bills, get out your invoices, and go to the gym three times a week.

Keeping Your Momentum Going

Few people can be productive for more than a couple of hours without at least a minor change of pace, task, or scenery. It's fine occasionally to get up for a snack, water the plants, or bring in the mail. As long as you're not trying to avoid work, you can even throw in a load of laundry or mow the grass or phone a friend. Sometimes we need a change of stimulus or to get our blood moving. In fact, if you are stuck on a problem, the most effective way to get unstuck may be to put it on the back burner for a while. However, you must be able to distinguish between controlled breaks and distractions. Throwing in a load of laundry is fine, but this is not the time do to a top-to-bottom housecleaning. Don't phone a friend to whom you can never talk for less than an hour.

A minor change of scenery can help—sit in a different chair to read that trade journal, take the laptop to the back porch to get some fresh air, or have a quick jog around the block. Taking a break can be as simple as eating lunch looking out the window rather than eating at your desk.

Many of the distractions home workers fall prey to result from their own weaknesses. Help yourself by limiting temptations. Don't have a TV in the room you use as an office. Put away anything not related to your work—kids' toys, the novel you're reading. Make sure your office is pleasant, well lit, and has a chair with good back support. While many people love working in their sweats, others need to dress up in order to be in the working mind-set. It's very important to exercise regularly, preferably in the early morning. I recommend going to a gym because it gets you out of the house.

People Distractions

Other distractions come from family, friends, and neighbors. While working from a home office is common enough now that most people "get it," there are still a few people who assume they can drop in just to chat. It's up to you to educate them and set limits. Make it clear that you're working and won't be available until after 5:00. If you're committed to what you're doing, this isn't hard.

I don't buy the "my friend means well, I don't want to hurt her feelings" argument. You must confront this situation head-on and have a talk with your friend. Make sure he or she knows that this is your job and you are serious about making it work. A real friend who means well will change his or her behavior. A true friend wants you to succeed.

Scheduling

Avoid rush-hour traffic and stores' busy periods. If your work requires lots of uninterrupted time to think, and you are disciplined enough, confine client meetings to two days each week so you have the other three days to work without interruption. On the other hand, if being alone that much gets you down, spread out your client meetings so you get out briefly every day. Save trips by scheduling your doctor checkup on the way home from Monday's client meeting, go to the gym after your Tuesday meeting, do the grocery shopping on Wednesday, and so forth.

This way, you get out every day but still avoid unnecessary trips. If you do personal things during the day, you must work some evening hours, so you're putting in eight hours a day. But if your schedule is too rigid, you won't stick to it. Your schedule should make your life easier, not more complicated. Play with it until you find what works for you.

Getting Going in the Morning

How do you make sure you get up at a reasonable hour when no one's expecting you at the office at 9:00 A.M.? There are lots of ways. Your business may dictate your hours. If you have employees who ring your doorbell at 9:00, or you're a telecommuter whose boss calls at 8:30, it's taken care of. If you're a consultant with a partner across town, you could have daily phone meetings at 9:00 A.M. You can create your own "starting bell": Start work as soon as your spouse leaves for work or your kids leave for school. Some people create rituals: A financial planner puts on his suit and tie, leaves by the front door, walks to the corner to buy the *Wall Street Journal,* scans the headlines while walking back, and when he returns home, he enters through the back door, which leads directly to his office.

How to Stop Working

Just as there are people who have trouble starting in the morning, there are people who can't *stop* working. You may need some kind of ritual to help you quit work. It's easier to separate work and personal time if your office is in a separate wing of the house. You can close the office door, walk away, and not see the room again until the next morning. If the layout of your home precludes a physical separation, you'll need to create an end-of-day ritual: A graphic designer leaves her computer, goes out the side door to the garage, opens and closes the car door, then goes to the front door and so "comes home."

It's more complicated when your line of work makes it impossible to stop at 5:00 or 6:00 P.M. If you're a therapist who works evenings, if you give seminars on Saturdays, or if you often travel out of town, you face a challenge. You must be available when business beckons, but you don't want to work around the clock, month in, month out. The solution is to plan in advance to block out personal time. Instead of having time to yourself the same evening every week, you'll have it at different times throughout the month. Plan ahead and guard this time like it's an appointment. Put an X through it in your planner so business doesn't encroach. Better yet, make a nonwork appointment—a date with your spouse or a visit with a friend. Commit yourself to weekend getaways by making reservations and paying in advance.

Kids and the Home Office

People who decide to work at home so they can see their kids more or cut child care costs are almost always disappointed. They find that they get very little work done with small children around, and they end up arranging for in-home care or sending the kids back to day care. You can't get work done if your kids have continual access to you during working hours. Set up some rules about when you will and won't be available.

Make child care arrangements to cover most of your working hours, perhaps through a baby-sitter or shared child care arrangements with other home office workers in your neighborhood. Make it clear to your family that if it's something they wouldn't call you at the office for, they shouldn't interrupt you just because you're in the den. You should be no more accessible than when you worked at an outside office. Yes, you will gain more time to spend with your family, but it's the time you formerly spent commuting—not time subtracted from earning a living.

Paul and Sarah Edwards, nationally known experts on home-based business, explain that "since your family is probably used to having you generally accessible when you're at home, discovering they can't talk to you during large blocks of time can be quite an adjustment. . . . Work out a clear plan with your family and get their support. Let them know when you will be working and what your expectations of them are during that time. The plan should define the following:

1. How everyone will know when you are working and when you aren't. How you'll signal your family that this is work time.
2. When you are not to be interrupted, the particular hours or activities.
3. What other expectations you have: Any areas of the house that must be kept neat. The sound level you expect in the house while you're working. Who is responsible for managing household events while you are

working. Whether you expect anyone else, such as a spouse or older child, to be responsible for making sure you aren't interrupted. Whether you want anyone to answer your business phone. Whether you have any particular expectations for them when you have business visitors.

4. How any young children will be cared for while you are working."

Plan your work schedule around important family activities, suggests C. J. Hayden, a San Francisco business coach and author of *Get Clients Now!* If your kids get home at 2:00, work from 8:30 to 2:00 and 4:00 to 6:00. Decide how many hours you want to work, draw up a schedule, then post it on your office door so your family knows when you'll be available.

Sharing Household Chores

Instead of arbitrarily assigning household chores, ask each family member to volunteer. If there are lots of tasks left over, ask if they really need to be done, or done as often. (Maybe the living room could be vacuumed less often?) Make it clear that you expect everyone to do his or her share. When someone doesn't do an assigned chore, don't back down and do it yourself. This sets a bad precedent and makes it even less likely your family will do their share in the future. "Serving a meal on dirty dishes may seem extreme, but it gets the message across," Hayden says.

Hold up your end of the bargain, too. If you tell your kids to wait until 5:00, don't renege on that promise. Quit work then, or at least take a break and spend some time with them.

Don't let children answer the business phone. You don't want your client to be told that Daddy can't come to the phone because he's going poo-poo. Your client might find it endearing, but more likely he or she will wonder how you get any work done.

Find ways to involve your kids in aspects of your work that are age-appropriate: stuffing envelopes, bundling old boxes for recycling, straightening up your supply cabinet, taping shut shipping boxes.

Combatting Isolation

Depression is an occupational hazard of working at home because of the isolation and lack of stimulation. If you have your own business (as opposed to a telecommuter getting a salary), you have the added stressor of financial uncertainty.

Katherine Crowley, a therapist in New York City who specializes in the problems and challenges faced by self-employed people, says, "At The Business Strategy Seminars, we regularly work with clients whose business ideas never become reality because a lack of input made them prey to their greatest fears and doubts. We need social contact to maintain energy levels, generate ideas, and maintain perspective."

If you're an entrepreneur in a home office and you wish you had someone to talk to—someone besides the UPS man—you're not alone. In fact, the difficulties of working alone are so well recognized that a support community, the Let's Talk Business Network, was founded just to fill this need. Mitch Schlimer, one of the network's founders, is convinced that the alarmingly high failure rate of small business is largely due to the isolation that entrepreneurs feel.

Most everyone needs some social stimulation during the workday. When it's built into your environment, as it is at the office, you may underestimate how much you rely on it to keep your energy up. Even if you found the noise, interruptions, and politics of the corporate office stressful, you may be surprised to find that total isolation is even worse. Here are some ways to combat isolation.

- Join professional or trade organizations and attend their programs and lunches. Better yet, become active on a committee.
- Join networking groups to make business connections and share referrals.
- Join an entrepreneur's support group for brainstorming, moral support, and input.
- Schedule two business lunches a week with clients, people you meet networking, and neighborhood folks with home offices.
- A trip to the store or the health club can give you some energy, just so it's not an excuse to avoid working.
- Maintain your contacts with former co-workers. (Just don't give them the impression you have lots of time to phone them because you have no business—even if it's true.)
- Have a couple of supportive friends you can call to help get you moving. Make sure they are the sort of people who help you keep perspective as opposed to magnifying your worries about your business.
- Get out of the house at least once a day.

Successful Telecommuting

As companies try harder to retain their best employees, an increasing number allow employees to telecommute. According to a 1998 survey, 51 percent of North American companies now permit some sort of telecommuting, and experts expect the trend to continue. More than half of AT&T's white-collar workforce telecommutes at least two days a week.

Telecommuters share some issues with entrepreneurs, but there are key differences. Since you have a job, you get a predictable income and benefits, your company probably provides your equipment, and you'll have less latitude about structuring your days.

Telecommuting saves the companies money in the long run, but if done properly it costs more initially. They need to buy you a computer with modem, a second phone line to dial into the company network, a fax machine, and perhaps a third phone line for it. You'll also need remote access software to synchronize your home computer's files with those back at the office and tap into the office's computer network. This same remote access software will enable technicians at headquarters to dial into your computer via modem and repair it if you have a problem.

There are legal issues to address. Find out if your zoning permits home offices in your neighborhood. You will need to define clearly who's responsible for company equipment kept in your home office in case of theft. Find out what your homeowner's insurance policy covers.

While part of the appeal of telecommuting is flexibility, you need some structure for it to succeed. You and your employer must agree on how accessible you will be. You need to agree on certain hours you can be reached, how often you'll check your E-mail, and how to handle things like if you go take your kid to the dentist—will you be available by pager, or just announce on your voice mail when you'll be back? If you work some evenings, you need to have some predictable daytime hours so co-workers can reach you. Stay in the communications loop: If possible, attend staff meetings in person. Alternatively, you can hold meetings by teleconference. You're not limited to three people, because each person who joins can connect to two others.

The Merrill Lynch Story

While some companies have casual telecommuting arrangements, others have programs that are quite structured. Merrill Lynch's program is one of the most ambitious and comprehensive in the country. They require several months of applications, interviews, and formal training. Having a formal program addresses corporate concerns about liability, productivity, and fairness.

Prospective telecommuters are screened, then they must complete a training program. Only certain categories of workers are eligible. They must fill out a detailed application that states why they want to work at home (to avoid commuting five days a week—okay; to save on child care costs by watching the kids while you work—forget it) and what their schedule will be. After a series of meetings and interviews, prospective telecommuters spend two weeks in a simulation lab, working on a real project, on the same equipment they'll have at home. The simulation lab has large windows with a view, and a refrigerator around the corner to help workers learn to deal with distractions. They cannot walk down the hall to talk to co-workers, they must phone or E-mail them. The point is to simulate working remotely as accurately as possible.

Once the fledgling telecommuters are ready, they are given state-of-the-art laptops, printers, and fax machines. Their desks, chairs, and lighting must be ergonomically correct (they submit photographs of their home office for approval). Once they've moved home, they must document their hours worked and submit weekly progress reports. They have official starting times, ending times, lunch breaks, and specified times to check their E-mail. They must submit proof that they've arranged child care during work hours. They still have to be in the office at least one day a week and for staff meetings and people's birthdays.

Why is Merrill Lynch going to all this trouble and expense? When done with the right employees, it enhances productivity and enables the company to retain valuable workers by giving them the flexibility and support they want.

15

Home and Family

> *Managerial skills are every bit as important in our domestic*
> *and social concerns as they are in business concerns. . . . This*
> *is because every home requires managing. In fact, most*
> *homes require all the skills required by most offices.*
>
> —ALEC MACKENZIE

When your home is organized, it becomes an effective base of operations and a relaxing refuge. When it's not, it's an obstacle course. This is a given. The only question is: How organized can your home *realistically* be?

Don't be discouraged by stories of women who have jobs and four children and are always perfectly groomed and well rested and active on five civic committees and still have time to spare. Such women do exist, but in my experience, they not only have above-average supportive husbands, they also have the bucks to hire household help. If you don't have a nanny, a housekeeper, and a driver, don't beat yourself up comparing yourself to these "perfect" women.

Economist Juliet B. Shor asserts that, "The household has not yet caught up to the twentieth century. We have a society in which the routines of the household, and what's required, is something that was developed when you had a full-time housewife."

> Gail Blanke, former senior vice president of Avon Products, Inc., who left to run LifeDesigns, an organization designed to help women define and then live their dreams, has the following advice: "Living your dreams is good for your children, not bad for them. I have two daughters whom I am totally committed to. . . . The greatest gift we can give the people we love, and in particular our children, is to live the life of our dreams. That way we give them permission to live theirs."

Let Go of the Supermom Myth

Trying to be supermom is not only hard on you, it's hard on your family, too. They have to put up with you being exhausted, frazzled, and resentful. Giving up the quest for perfection doesn't mean lowering your standards, not at all. It frees your time and energy to do a few selected things even better. Research done in 1994 by the Families and Work Institute found that what kids want from their parents is not more time, but for their parents to be less stressed, even if it means the parents spend less time with them.

Your first step is to reexamine the number of belongings you "must" own and the things you "must" do and find areas where you can simplify. This will cut down on housework and maintenance. The more stuff you have, the more effort it takes to maintain it all. Everything has three price tags: what you pay for it, the space required to keep it, and the cost of maintaining it. (See Chapter 8, "The Perils of Stuff," and Chapter 3, "How Do You Want to Spend Your Time?")

Next, examine your housekeeping standards. Being less of a perfectionist about keeping a perfect home will give you more time to enjoy life. Could you clean a little less often? Maybe you haven't had people over in years because you "have" to redecorate first, then of course prepare an elaborate meal. Why not just invite a few close friends over for a potluck? They won't care that you still have the same sofa you had last time or the bathroom rug doesn't match the towels. Their homes aren't perfect either! A casual gathering is better than never seeing anybody because you don't have time to make things perfect.

Just because you've always done it a certain way doesn't mean you can't change it. Remember, it's you who chooses. Make your choices consciously. Here are some ways you can gain time by simplifying.

- If you have a long commute, try to get a job closer to home, or arrange to work at home one to two days a week.
- Your home should suit the amount of time you want to spend on maintenance. If you're still living

in a four-bedroom house decades after your kids have left the nest, consider moving to a smaller house.

- Same goes for your yard. If maintaining your huge lawn and garden has become a burden, replace high-maintenance with low- or no-maintenance plants. Or you could cut maintenance time down to nothing by landscaping with wood chips, rocks, or ground cover.
- If you can get just one more use out of something before washing it, you'll cut down on the time you spend doing laundry. Can you use a towel once more before washing it?
- Laundry is even more time-consuming if you are an apartment dweller and use a commercial laundromat. Buy extra sheets, towels, and so on, so you can make the trip less often. It's a waste of time to do laundry every weekend.

Taking Care of You

Don't forget to take time for a very important person—you. Being there for those who need you doesn't mean you should be a doormat. Reserve some time to call your own and *never* give it away to anyone else unless it's a real emergency. You can read, exercise, or soak in the bathtub. Let your family know that this is your time and you are not to be interrupted. If you feel guilty spending time on yourself because it takes time away from your family, remember that if you become burned out or sick, you'll have even less time to take care of your family.

New York therapist and career counselor Barbara Sher describes an exercise she does with women in her time-management workshops. She calls it the "Love Showdown." Sher urges overworked moms to "choose one activity you are going to give up every day—and replace it with something you love to do. You could choose to stop shopping, chauffeuring your kids to the pool, or taking your husband's clothes to the cleaners. It has to give you at least thirty minutes a day for yourself, and that thirty minutes has to be spent doing something that is only for you." Initially the women were too stunned to speak, then one woman stood up and said she'd stop ironing shirts, another stood up and said she'd give up typing everybody's school papers, and after a while they were all buzzing with conspiratorial excitement. To protect them against the guilt they were sure to feel if their families complained, Sher had them write down a little speech that they would say: "I shop and cook and make your beds and drive you places and earn money to share with you and I do it all with pleasure because I love you. I want your minds to be free to study and to do your personal work and to have a great life. What I want to know is, do you love me enough to let me have a half-hour a day for the same thing, *or do you love dinner more?* If you love dinner more, I really ought to know that." Barbara Sher says, "It's time to wake up the mamas *and their families* too." She recommends putting a sign on the refrigerator: "In this house, everybody gets what they need, even Mom."

Quality Time for the Family

There's a lot to be said for reducing time spent watching TV. It means more quality time for the family or solo activities. Your kids' grades will improve and they will develop new hobbies. Less exposure to advertising lessens the temptation to buy things you can't afford and don't need. Perhaps you and your spouse always watch TV together every night. Is this necessary to keep your marriage together? Instead, you could do household chores and pay bills in the evenings, leaving the weekend free. Some families have an embargo on TV from Sunday evening until the following Friday evening. You could even get rid of your television altogether—people have done this and survived.

Designate certain time periods free of phone calls, incoming or outgoing. Tell friends, neighbors, and business associates that you're not available on, say, Wednesday evenings. Ask them to call at other times, and screen calls through your answering machine so you can pick up if there's an emergency.

To make sure you spend quality time with your spouse, make a date for every Saturday night, and have a standing arrangement with a sitter whom you've booked well in advance for that night.

An increasing number of employers offer some type of flexible scheduling for their workers. This isn't good only for parents of young children. If you have a sick elderly parent, you may be able to work at home one day a week to make it easier to drive Dad to the doctor. If your boss is reluctant, point out that it'll be less disruptive to your job than you having to leave the office midday to check in on Dad or drive him to the doctor, plus being distracted with worries even when you're there all day.

Working Dads

A 1997 survey by the Families and Work Institute found of the 2,877 working parents interviewed, 63 percent wished they could reduce the number of hours they worked, and 70 percent of them did not have enough time to spend with their children.

The plight of working mothers is well documented, but only recently is attention being paid to the father as anything more than a breadwinner. Fathers, too, are frustrated by work schedules that keep them away from their kids, perhaps doubly frustrated because they're traditionally not supposed to care about such things. "We haven't even developed a concept of the working father," notes James Levine, director of the institute's Fatherhood Project. A decade ago nobody talked about fathers being torn between the demands of family and work, and fathers were afraid they'd be passed over for promotion if they complained about their long work hours or tried to avoid a heavy travel schedule.

When Levine first started his work in 1990, he was afraid no fathers would show up—but they came in droves, relieved at being able to talk, at last, about their desire to be there for their families and still succeed at work. Levine's seminar, "DaddyStress: How Fathers and Managers Can Deal Effec-

tively with Work-Family Conflict," has been extremely popular at corporations such as Merrill Lynch, American Express,
IBM, and Time Warner. Levine's mission is to convince
American business that offering flexible scheduling for parents
of both sexes is good for the bottom line. (He has the data to
back this up. Companies that offer family-supportive benefits
have more motivated employees and lower turnover.) Levine
feels that if men feel safe discussing their concern about
work/family balance, it will ultimately change society's perception of family issues from a "woman's issue" to everyone's issue.

Teaching Organization and Responsibility to Children

Have a weekly list of chores and assign every family member to
do his or her share. Rotate jobs so one person isn't always stuck
with cleaning out the cat box. There's no reason to restrict this
to older kids. Get the family together to discuss how everybody
can pitch in.

Georgene Lockwood, author of *The Complete Idiot's Guide
to Organizing Your Life,* says even "young children can learn to
help out at home. . . . Toddlers can learn to pick up their own
toys at night and adhere to a schedule. . . . This means working
with the child. A task may take longer at first, but you're not
only teaching, you're spending quality time with your child,
becoming closer and sharing experiences."

Children can set and clear the table, make beds, bundle up
the recycling, take care of the dog. Be consistent—you might
make a deal that they can't watch TV until the chores are done.
If a child doesn't do a job, don't do it for him or her. Don't be
a perfectionist. Be patient and praise your kids.

- Provide child-size tools that make it easy for children to help. Don't expect them to sweep the dining room or shovel snow with adult-sized tools.
- Buy colorful baskets to make it fun for kids to put away their toys.
- Use clear or colored plastic boxes to store toys on shelves.
- To make it easy for kids to put things away, label boxes with words and pictures. Glue part of the photo from the box it came in to the front of the storage box, so kids know what goes where.
- Use small baskets to store similar toys together.
- Put shelves low enough that children can reach them.
- Hang clothes low enough that kids can reach to hang up their own clothes. Keep hats, scarves, mittens, boots, and umbrellas in baskets by the door. (This not only reduces household clutter but also saves getting-ready time because people don't have to look high and low to find what they need.)
- Give each child a plastic bin to hold personal-care items, then arrange bins on the bathroom shelf.
- Paint "parking spaces" on the garage floor for kids' bikes, wagons, lawn mower, wheelbarrow, etc. This makes it fun for kids to put away their things.

Professional organizer Barbara Hemphill sees many overwhelmed, frustrated adults who try to do too much, unable to make choices and decisions. Because coping in today's world requires making choices, Hempill feels that we have an obligation to teach our children organizing skills. We can begin with teaching them how to handle their school papers and calendars. If a child needs a ride to a school event, have her write it on the calendar. This teaches her to take responsibility for herself. The calendar can also be used to teach long-term planning and goal setting, such as by breaking homework projects into weekly or daily quotas; taking a trip next summer means earning *x* amount of baby-sitting money each week. Older children can start filing their papers. Do whatever you can to make the organizing process appeal to your child, such as using bright colored folders or containers.

Minimizing Morning Misery

To minimize chaos in the morning, prepare the night before. Lay out kids' clothes and your own as well, pack a day care bag, prepare school lunches. To make it easier for kids to dress themselves, fold and store entire outfits together (everything except shoes) in the drawer. Backpacks and briefcases should be repacked each night and placed by the front door. When you repack the backpack with books and finished homework, jot on the calendar any field trip dates or items your child must bring to school. Save time for yourself too by hanging outfits together, so you don't have to scramble in the morning for what goes together. To save time and prevent bickering over "borrowed" barrettes and brushes, give each family member his or her own colorful basket for bathroom supplies.

⏰ Keeping Your Home Under Control

- If you tend to lose your keys, keep them on a hook by the door.
- Establish a to-do area by the door for everything that needs to go out—to photocopy, take to the cleaners, give to a friend, return to the library.
- Keep a basket at the foot of the steps for items that belong upstairs.
- Keep a basket on the upstairs landing for things to be taken downstairs.
- If you can't bring items to their final destinations as soon as you get home, designate a processing area where such things (receipts and warranties for newly purchased items, mail, and so forth) are put temporarily.
- If you have a messy spouse, don't try to change him. Allow him to be messy but confined to one area.

Roberta Roesch, author of *Time Management for Busy People*, says that older children can help younger children get dressed. As soon as children are old enough, enforce a rule that they don't leave their rooms until they're dressed and their beds are made. Have everyone rinse his or her own dishes and put them in the dishwasher.

Operations Central

Every family needs a place for processing mail and paying bills. Ideally, it should be a small desk that's permanent and not used for anything else—not the kitchen table. You need an uncluttered surface to write on. Stock it with a calendar, scissors, pencil, pens, highlighter, tape, stapler, envelopes, address stickers, stamps, calculator, notepaper, paper clips, letter opener, bank deposit slips, and sticky notes. It must be near the phone—many pieces of paper can be eliminated immediately with a phone call. Your processing area also needs a filing cabinet (perhaps on rollers), good lighting, a comfortable chair, a speakerphone (so you can be productive while you're on hold), and a wastebasket. Open mail in the same place every day so it doesn't get strewn everywhere.

You also need a tickler file with slots for each date of the month (see Chapter 5, "Managing Your Desktop"). This holds concert announcements, bills to be paid, dry cleaning tickets, receipts for items to be returned to the store, greeting cards to mail, and more.

In addition, you could have a file for each family member. Keep children's papers in order by labeling a file folder for each child. Permission slips, lunch money, and concert and sports schedules can be kept there.

To make sure phone messages get passed on and activity schedules are not lost, divide a bulletin board into sections with a space labeled for each family member. Use a phone message book like those used in offices—if the original you tear off is lost, you have the backup carbonless copy still in the book.

Lisa lived in a small apartment with her nine-year-old daughter, Mikki. She had trouble maintaining order on her desk because Mikki dumped her stuff on the same desk. Because mother and daughter shared the desk—both of them used it for the computer—Mikki didn't understand that Mommy didn't want her schoolbooks all over the desk when she was paying bills. The solution was to get a separate small table for Mikki's use only. Now that Mikki has her very own little desk, Lisa has her desk back.

Generally it's best to use the same calendar for both personal and work appointments; this prevents you from scheduling yourself to be in two places at the same time. However, if you have young children, you need to keep a large calendar at home as well (probably in the kitchen) to keep track of everyone's school events, field trips, sports practice, music lessons, and birthday parties. When Mike brings home his schedule for basketball practice, he can promptly enter the dates on the family calendar. Mom and Dad do the same when they're scheduled for business trips. Make a copy of the family calendar to carry with you during the day. This will prevent last-minute panics about who will drive Mike to basketball practice. Making copies is easy if you keep the calendar in the computer. Print out three copies: one for the kitchen, one for you, and one for your spouse. Have a family meeting each Sunday evening to go over everyone's schedule and make sure that child care and chauffeuring children to their activities is covered and that an adult will be home each evening.

When you draw up instructions for child care providers, make several copies at one time. Keep it in the computer for easy updating. Do the same with your packing list for your summer vacation or camping trips.

Getting Help

If you can't keep up with the housework, ask your family for more help—and don't wait until you're about to crack. You may be afraid to ask your children to help, but they probably prefer chipping in to you being exhausted and crabby and having no time to relax with the family because you're busy being supermom. (The same goes for single dads.)

Start a baby-sitting co-op in your neighborhood. Even if you normally use a day care center, you should have a sitter for backup—if your kid's coming down with something, you don't have to take him or her to day care and expose the others. Have a list of several reliable baby-sitters, with references checked in advance, so if one arrangement falls through you have several other options.

Set up carpools with your children's friends' parents. One parent can pick up and drive all the kids to band practice one week and you can do it the next, which gives each of you a free evening.

Consider outsourcing tasks—mowing the grass, shoveling walks, running errands, yard work, housecleaning, laundry, washing the car, household repairs, meal preparation, and grocery shopping can all be hired out. Ask neighborhood teenagers. Check newspaper classifieds, bulletin boards in grocery stores, weekly newspapers, and shopper publications. You can also try the employment office of a local high school or college. It's common nowadays to pay people to do things such as stand in line for you to buy tickets or wait for deliveries.

Creative Ways to Get Help

Any of the above chores can be traded with a neighbor or friend. If you hate grocery shopping and your neighbor hates cleaning, let her shop for you and you'll clean for her. You can apply this principle to all kinds of things. It's especially useful for single people: You can mend your friend's coat if he'll put up that shelf you need.

Ruth Klein, author of *Where Did the Time Go? A Working Woman's Guide to Creative Time Management*, recommends creating your own extended family, a group of backup people you know you can rely on in a real emergency. This is not to be abused for routine child care or minor favors; it's understood that in times of crisis, they'll come running. This is especially useful for single parents. It could be a retired nurse you hire to care for a sick child when you absolutely can't miss work. It could be a widow who'd love to have a relationship with a family and needs extra cash. Or you can pay by returning favors.

A Closet That Works

A messy closet wastes your time when you're getting ready in the morning, prevents you from looking your best, and causes you to waste money by buying more clothes than you really need. Your closet should contain only clothes that look and feel good and are in good condition—and still fit. If it's not wearable, it shouldn't be in your closet.

I recommend a complete closet excavation. Set aside time to do it all at once; perhaps a Saturday—this can't be done in bits and pieces. Make arrangements in advance for Salvation Army pickup—this forces you to follow through with it. Enlist the help of a friend with good taste; she can tell you what's hopelessly unflattering and what merely needs a different belt and shoes.

Take everything out of your closet. Divide articles of clothing into four piles: the discards, items that would be fine were they cleaned or mended, items you wear often, and items that fit you and are in good shape but you don't know what to wear them with.

The discards pile should include anything that no longer fits or is out of date, unflattering, uncomfortable, or stained or damaged beyond repair. Unless it's very special, get rid of anything you haven't worn in two years. Discard uncomfortable shoes—you'll never wear them. Most of these can be given to charity. This pile should include the scarf or hat you've never worn that was a gift from your cousin. If you want to, wear it once so your cousin sees you in it, then donate it so a needy person can use it.

Any items needing to be dry-cleaned or have buttons replaced or the hem fixed should be placed in the car now (make a note in your planner to go to the cleaner or tailor).

The third pile contains outfits you wear often. See if you can get even more mileage from these. Try them on, experiment with accessories. You're sure to discover new combinations; have your friend take photos when you do. Now you can put the garments back into the closet. You'll hang the photos of the new combos inside your closet door to save time dressing in the morning.

The fourth pile contains clothing you like and that fits, but you're not sure if it goes with anything. Try on these pieces in various combinations and use your imagination. You're bound to discover great outfits you hadn't thought of before, and it

> You can simplify getting dressed by always wearing red, white, blue, or black—everything goes together!

won't cost you a penny! (This is where your friend with the good taste comes in.) Again, have your friend take photos of your newly discovered combinations, and mount these photos inside your closet door, too.

What's left are the orphan pieces that you like and that still fit and flatter you: The becoming blouse that needs a skirt to go with it; an attractive but plain dress that would look much better with the right belt and shoes. Start a shopping list. As you study the possibilities of each garment, you realize that if you bought that skirt, a belt, shoes, and a few other things, you'd have several new outfits at very little cost. (Anything you don't think worth spending money on to make into an outfit, get rid of.)

Now put the rest of your clothes back in the closet (except what goes to the cleaner, tailor, or charity). Hang compatible separates together to save dressing time. Accessories must be stored where you can see them, or you'll forget what you've got and get no use out them. Use clear plastic shoe boxes or large plastic bags to hold scarves and accessories. This lets you see what's inside without opening the bag.

Maintaining It

Before you store out-of-season clothes, launder and mend them. It's important to dry-clean woolens before storing for the summer because moths are attracted to perspiration. Also, stains you can't even see will darken and become permanent with time.

To maintain your new, orderly closet, when you undress at the end of each day, hang up your clothes promptly rather than dropping garments on chairs to hang up "later." Off of you, directly onto the hanger, and right into the closet! This not only keeps the room tidy but also keeps clothes fresher and eliminates touch-up ironing. And don't put any garment back into your closet unless it's wearable. If it's missing a button or needs cleaning, deal with it before you put it back in the closet. You'll save lots of time dressing in the morning when everything in the closet is wearable.

Photos

As soon as they come back from the developer, go through each batch of photos, discard the bad ones, and label or date the keepers before putting them away. Do it now! Photo buffs who put this off end up with *hundreds* of photos—the good mixed in with the duds—to go through "later." Don't make more work for yourself down the road.

Ordering reprints is easier now that many photo developers offer contact sheets similar to those used by professional photographers. Instead of peering through strips of negatives searching for the one you want, you can pay a little more to have contact sheets made when you first have the film developed. This makes selecting the right negative fast and easy.

If you want to make duplicates of old family photos and preserve them for posterity, try making color photocopies.

🕐 Kids' Artwork

Rather than saving all of it forever, let your child choose his or her favorites and keep only those. Send the rest to the grandparents, or use them for wrapping paper.

Holidays

Catalogs are great time savers for holiday gift buying. Ask your spouse and kids to look through their favorite catalogs and sign their names by items they want. This not only spares you having to fight the holiday crowds at the mall, but everybody gets what he or she wants, so there's nothing to exchange later.

Collaborate on holiday baking. A group of friends or neighbors can agree that each will bake a large amount of a particular cookie and share it with the group. This way each person has a wide variety of treats with a fraction of the effort because each makes only one recipe.

If you're one of the many people who find the holiday hubbub exhausting and feel drained in January, you may be ready for more drastic measures. Who says you have to spend three weeks at the end of every year in a frenzy of shopping, visiting, baking, buying, sending cards to people you scarcely know because they sent you a card last year, cleaning, buying outfits you'll wear only once, gift wrapping, attending holiday concerts, then returning unwanted gifts? When you rush from one activity to another, no wonder you don't enjoy it. For many people, the holidays means spending precious vacation time with relatives they don't enjoy (or even dislike), spending money for things they can't afford, and beginning the new year mentally and financially depleted. Why not take back the holidays and celebrate in more enjoyable ways?

Dianna Booher, author of *Get a Life Without Sacrificing Your Career*, suggests, "If you're dreading the holidays because of the hassles, consider simplifying the system. Announce your decision early to your family so they can make adjustments in their plans. Then focus on the spiritual significance and forget all the meaningless, tiresome trappings. . . . You notice I didn't say skip the fun, rest, or spirit of the holidays—only the hassles. For the last several years, our extended family has opted for meeting at the mall, pooling our family gift-giving money, and donating it for a needy family (paying their rent for a month, taking them a tree, and buying gifts for their kids). Not only have we cut down on our family shopping time, but we've had a chance to spend time together as a family and do a little good for someone else."

Tips for Saving Time at Home

- Don't run out of any staple item. Replace things before you run out. Buy in bulk things like toilet paper and shampoo. (It's also cheaper.)
- Shop at off-hours when stores are less crowded.
- Buy lots of panty hose when they're on sale. For men, dress shirts and socks.
- Don't buy or subscribe to more magazines and newspapers than you can read. *Never* start a magazine subscription just because it's on sale or free.
- Do errands in groups by neighborhood to minimize travel time.
- Don't buy clothes that need to be ironed after laundering. Avoid buying clothes that need to be cleaned every second wearing.
- Keep a small notebook in your pocket or purse to jot reminders to yourself.
- Use the answering machine to screen calls.
- Use a speaker- or cordless phone so you can fold laundry, empty the dishwasher, or straighten up the living room while you talk.
- Lower your housecleaning standards. If you're

exhausted, catching up on your sleep is more important than mopping the kitchen floor. Stop being a perfectionist.
- Watch less television.
- Triple each recipe you make. All this takes is planning ahead when you shop, and a large freezer.
- If you haven't used a recipe within a month, the odds you'll ever use it are very slim, so toss it. There will be many more recipes.
- Use binders with clear plastic page holders to hold clipped recipes. You can read recipes without pulling them out of a file, and they're spill-resistant.
- Stop sending holiday cards except to a small, select group of people.

Important Papers

Every adult needs to keep important papers in order so that in case of emergency or death, the family can quickly find critical information. While it's hard to confront these things, it's really an act of love to make it easier on your family if something bad happens. Draw up a master list that indicates the location of:

- birth certificate
- citizenship papers
- military and veteran papers
- marriage license
- bank records
- insurance policies
- investment records
- title to the car

- deed to the house
- pension or retirement information
- power of attorney
- location of safe-deposit box, its number, and key
- social security number and records
- tax records
- will

Your master list should indicate not only the location of each of these documents; it should also list bank account numbers; car registration; important names, addresses, and phone numbers (doctor, lawyer, accountant); social security number; and driver's license number. Keep more than one copy of the list; perhaps one in a safe-deposit box or at your accountant's and the other at home. A fireproof box or safe is a good idea for the master list and also for important papers you'd rather not put in a safe-deposit box, such as family historical information and photos. If there are irreplaceable papers that you must keep close at hand, store a duplicate copy off-site.

Videotape your possessions and store the tape off-site, so if you lose your home you don't lose your proof for insurance as well. Find out if your insurance company also insists on original receipts; if so, store receipts for major purchases off-site.

A trusted adult should have power of attorney so someone can handle your affairs if you become incapacitated.

🕘 How Long Should I Save It?

Credit Card Charge Slips These need to be saved only until the monthly statement arrives. Look it over when you pay the bill. Because you generally can't return items after thirty days have passed, the only reason to save charge slips after that is for major purchases, tax-deductible expenses, and employer-reimbursable expenses. Save receipts and charge slips for expensive items like washers and dryers to back up their warranties.

Bank Accounts After you verify the accuracy of each monthly statement, discard the cash withdrawal slips. Save only deposit slips and monthly statements and store these with your tax records for that year. Note on each deposit slip the source of the deposit. If you're audited by the IRS, they'll treat all deposits as taxable income unless you can prove otherwise.

Tax Records and Documentation The IRS has three years from the date you filed your return—or its due date (including any extensions), whichever is later—in which to audit your return. If they audit, they'll ask to see a copy of the preceding year's return as well. Ross Wisdom, a C.P.A. with Kimerling, Margulies & Wisdom, Ltd., in New York City, recommends you keep all backup documentation (W-2s, 1099s, canceled checks for deductible expenses, records of investments and dividends, etc.) for five years. For example, 1998 records can be discarded in 2003, assuming you filed for 1998 on time.

If there are years for which you haven't filed, keep all records and backup documentation for those years regardless of how much time has passed. Then, after you file those years, keep the records and backup documentation for the five years after the date you filed, Wisdom suggests.

After five years you can toss out the backup documentation (bank records, canceled checks, and so on), but you may want to save a copy of each tax return for your own reference. Most accountants will keep copies of your tax returns. If you do your own taxes, keep a second copy of your returns off-site, perhaps in a safe-deposit box.

Investments Keep year-end statements.

Home Keep records of sale or purchase of a home. Also keep records of home improvement expenses, as these are deducted from the gains when you sell.

Insurance Policies Keep current policies, as well as previous policies, in case of unresolved claims.

Contracts Keep any contracts still in force. For contracts that have expired, ask your attorney.

Health Records In addiction to your current health insurance policy, keep records of out-of-pocket medical expenses for two years. If you have substantial medical expenses, these may have tax implications as well. If you switch insurers you may need proof that you were previously insured and that it didn't lapse, so save proof of your former policy until your new one is securely in place.

Save These Permanently Birth, marriage, divorce, and death certificates; military papers; stock and bond records; papers documenting home purchases and improvements; year-end brokerage and mutual fund statements; stock option agreements; wills and trust agreements; and IRA records.

When you receive your monthly bank statement, check your record of transactions against the bank's record. But it's not just mistakes in your own ledger you're looking for. According to C.P.A. Ross Wisdom, banks make a lot of errors, so you should reconcile your bank statement each month.

Photocopy your driver's license, credit cards, insurance cards, and social security card. Arrange them on the copy machine glass and copy all on one page. Keep a copy at your office and one at home. This will come in handy if your wallet is stolen or lost.

Keep duplicates of keys at a friend's or neighbor's house, in case you're locked out.

For household appliances, staple receipts to the warranty card or user's manual, jot down the date and place of purchase, and store with other manuals and warranties in an accordion file. A good place to keep this file is the kitchen. (If the purchase is tax-deductible, better to file the original receipt with tax papers and keep the copy in the kitchen file.)

16

New Habits for a New Life

Every decision is an opportunity to gain some control over your future. However, when you put off decisions you are forfeiting that opportunity. Sooner or later circumstances will prevail and your right of choice will be taken away. By being indecisive, you allow yourself to become a slave to your future rather than the master of it.

—MICHAEL LeBOEUF

By now, you've probably tried some of the techniques in this book and are eager to try more. Don't be discouraged if your initial attempts at time management don't bring wonderful results. It takes patience and persistence. No system works unless you stick with it. Experiment, find what works for you, then fine-tune it. The longer you work at it, the easier it gets, and the more it pays off. For most of us, change is not easy, but you'll be rewarded many times over.

Little Things Add Up

One of the most powerful things you can do is break the habit of leaving papers lying around to decide about later. They mount up faster than you'd expect. A client once told me, "I'd thought piles were dead things, but they're not. They grow, they get bigger, and the next thing you know, those 'baby' piles are 'having sex' when you're not looking, and lo and behold, new piles are hatched!" She's right! The solution is to deal with them as you go along—don't wait until your piles are out of control. At the end of each day, straighten up your desk. Review what did and didn't get done and make notes for tomorrow.

Don't Beat Yourself Up

That is the ideal we should strive for. Maintaining it every day, however, is another matter. Realistically, it's okay to have one section of your desk for things you haven't dealt with yet. Same goes for your home (preferably one corner, not an entire room). But don't let it get out of hand. Unprocessed paper and belongings should be confined to that one area, not strewn everywhere. Deal with it at least once a week, and make sure things don't linger there too long. Your clutter corner should not become a permanent home for things you never get around to dealing with.

Most people don't have time to file every day. The solution is to keep a to-file area on one corner of your desk and deal with it at least once a week. This way if you need to locate something you haven't filed yet, there's only one place it can be—the to-file pile. And by the way, when you spot a paper you no longer need in an existing file, throw it away *now*. Don't say "someday" you'll clean out the file—someday quickly becomes never.

Don't be tempted to move your old stuff off your desk and into your briefcase. Bags and briefcases can become dangerous pockets of procrastination. I've seen people turn briefcases into long-term storage facilities, carrying stuff around for months. When it gets too heavy to lift, they buy a second briefcase or empty it into their car. As you know, this only postpones the day of reckoning. Better to deal with it sooner rather than later.

No one feels in control every day. If you feel overwhelmed once in a while, that's normal. But if you feel overwhelmed constantly, you need to say no more often. Get clear on your priorities and act accordingly. It's not enough to set priorities mentally—you must live them. Make sure your time use reflects your priorities. When you have too many things to do, ruthlessly eliminate any items that don't support your goals or priorities. Every day, scrutinize your calendar and to-do list for things you can cross off without doing.

The Decisive Moment

We are controlled by habit—our habits and habits of those around us. While we feel we have little control, in truth there's a *decisive moment*. Maybe your downfall is morning phone interruptions, which prevent you from getting any work done at the office. If morning is your peak concentration time, you need to guard your mornings. Put an announcement on your voice mail that you're available for calls after 11:30. Or perhaps you come home and eat junk food instead of a nourishing dinner, then you feel sluggish for the rest of the evening. If you know this about yourself, the decisive moment is when you decide what to eat for dinner. You can change the whole evening if you eat a healthful dinner. Stock up on groceries so you have no excuses. Or maybe the decisive moment is turning on the TV when you get home from work. So give yourself an alternative. Treat yourself to some new, upbeat CDs, put the TV in the closet, tackle those long-postponed projects, and watch your morale soar!

Ideal Daily Habits

What would make the biggest difference to you? It might include getting enough sleep, taking phone calls only during certain hours, clearing off your desk at the end of the day, having healthful food in the house, saying no to things you don't have time for, and doing at least one thing toward your long-term goals every day. Make a list of your ideal daily habits and post it on your wall. It helps to tell supportive friends and co-workers of your campaign.

Change requires a real commitment—a New Year's resolution or a gesture to placate a disgruntled spouse isn't enough. But if you are serious about regaining control of your life, major change is possible. In fact, the more frustrated you are with the status quo, the more motivated you'll be to change. I know it may seem impossible: How can you spend time doing these new things when you don't have a minute to spare? Initially, it *does* take time to save time. But every hour you invest now will be repaid many times over.

Take exercise as an example. If you're sluggish from eating poorly and a sedentary lifestyle, taking time to make healthful meals and go to the gym seems inconceivable—where will you find the time? You're already exhausted. But that's *why* you're exhausted. Once you start taking care of yourself, you'll have more time and energy. You'll move faster and sleep less. The hardest part is getting started.

It's the same with learning to manage your time. It's hard only at first—then you begin to see the results and you get excited. The longer you stick with it, the greater the payoff. This doesn't mean you'll never slack off. But once you've created a system and formed new habits, it's easy to restore order after a lapse.

> Discipline is the difference between success and failure. Earl Nightingale, a founder of the Nightingale-Conant Corporation, said, "The secret of success is that successful people form the habit of doing what failures don't want to do. What are these things? They are the very things that none of us, successes or failures, really like to do. Yet successful people do them anyway. . . . They do these things because they like the results they obtain. Failures, by contrast, tend to accept whatever results they get by doing only the things they like to do."

I believe deeply in people's capacity to change. I've seen many people go from continual crisis mode to having things under control and spending their time effectively. The hardest part is getting started. Then you begin to reap the benefits, which makes it easier to maintain your new habits. Once you start running your life instead of letting it run you, there will be no turning back. So go to it!

Before and After—A Time Makeover

Before—A Typical Day

You change clothes three times before finding a suit that's clean and fits well. Getting Suzie dressed is a struggle. Your husband is almost as bad because he's run out of dress shirts. Fortunately your husband is driving Suzie to the doctor today—you're already late for work. Uh-oh, where's Suzie's HMO referral form? You know you left it out in plain sight. But it's nowhere to be found.

Finally, you're out the door. You'll have forty minutes to read and do paperwork on the commuter train. You haven't culled your pile of newsletters and magazines, and every day your briefcase gets heavier. It now weighs about twenty pounds. You look for something to read on the train, but your "reading pile" is mostly junk mail and things that never should have left your desk. Whoa, *there* are those papers your client insisted he'd sent you. You just called him yesterday to ask where they were! Your briefcase contains several things that require action, but since you don't have supplies with you, they'll have to wait until you get to the office.

At the office, your morning, when you're most alert, is frittered away by interruptions and routine administrative tasks. Finally in the afternoon you tackle the Big Report that's due tomorrow. You have set aside today to deal with it. Now you realize that you need to track down some information. You make some phone calls and learn that the two people you must talk to are both away for the week. Your report will be late! Then, all afternoon people stream into your office asking questions—they weren't kept up to date and some of your instructions were not clear. But the real problem is that a serious error was just discovered in the Big Marketing Project. Some of the numbers don't add up. It wouldn't have been serious had it been discovered earlier. But at this stage, it's bad. You consider calling a meeting to make out a game plan, but everyone hates meetings so much, and there's really no time. As you hunt for the Big Marketing Project file, you discover a memo stating that the period for enrolling in the new health insurance is—oh no, was yesterday.

When you get home you're too tired to go to that free concert your friend invited you to. You didn't really want to go, but you felt you should because it was free, and you didn't want to hurt your friend's feelings by saying that you don't like folk music. Now you've got a terrible headache so you have an excuse to call her and cancel. Your friend wishes she'd known sooner so she could have given the ticket to someone else. Now you feel guilty.

The TV is blaring in the next room. Well, at least your kids are safe at home. You take some aspirin, then open your briefcase and try to figure out what to do about errors in the Big Marketing Project. Maybe you should tackle it Saturday when you're fresher, but you remember that you have a day full of errands to do Saturday. You force yourself to confront the project, your head still throbbing. The phone rings and you answer it—what if somebody needs you? One telemarketer, then a second. The third ring, it's someone you actually know, your gossipy cousin calling to dish the dirt on the relatives. You tell him you don't feel well and actually manage to get him off the phone in forty-five minutes (he usually runs on for an hour, so this is progress). Next thing you know the evening is over.

After—An Ideal Day

You get dressed in a flash because everything in your closet fits you. Suzie's outfit was laid out the night before, so getting her dressed is easy. Your husband has not run out of dress shirts because he buys them in multiples. You go to the kitchen and open the family tickler file. Under today's date is Suzie's doctor referral for her appointment today.

You'll have forty minutes to read on the train, so you pick up your folder of reading material. You cull it a couple times a week so everything in there is worth reading. You read several articles, and in the ten minutes you have left, you write a couple of thank-you cards to clients—easily done because cards, addresses, and stamps are right in your briefcase.

You're at your best in the morning, so you've scheduled from 9:00 to 12:00 to work on the Big Report, and you've told your secretary to protect you from interruptions. You have an appointment—with yourself. Because you've been dropping pertinent information into a folder for the past two months, you have everything you need to complete the Big Report in one sitting. That's a good thing, because Joe, your main information source, is out sick this week. But you spoke to him two weeks ago and got what you needed. You start to write the report at 9:00 A.M. and are done by noon.

However, a problem has been discovered in the Big Marketing Project. Some of the sales figures from last year don't add up. Fortunately it was caught early, at a preplanned checkpoint, so the damage is minor. There have been only a couple of interruptions today because you've kept people updated and your instructions were clear. The meeting is finished in only twenty-five minutes—careful planning of the agenda and selection of attendees pay off. People come to your meetings with ideas for solutions to problems, not just to complain, so they leave feeling encouraged. When you return to your office, an alarm goes off in your computer-scheduling software—the deadline for switching to the better health insurance plan is a week away. You make a phone call to take care of it now.

You spend a half hour at the end of the day planning. You do two errands on the way home. You're tired, but you know that if you do a little every day, Saturday will be free! When you get home you use your answering machine to screen calls. Thursday is your family's quiet evening. You have the volume turned up so you can hear if someone calls with an emergency. There's your cousin calling again to gossip about the relatives. You're glad the answering machine is on. After an hour of TV, your kids turn to their respective hobbies. The house is quiet and you have a relaxing evening with your family!

🕐 The Satisfaction of Completions

Business book author Jeff Davidson is a firm believer in the importance of completions, whether big or small. Ever notice how even putting away the dishes or taking out the garbage makes you feel good? The satisfaction of completions is even more important with bigger projects. When you complete something you feel a real sense of satisfaction and you take a mental break, however brief. It's a good foundation for what's next. On the other hand, when you leave tasks uncompleted—or finish, then race to the next project without acknowledging your accomplishments or even clearing off your desk—some of your emotional energy remains tied up in the last project. You've missed out on the satisfaction and mental clarity that a completion brings, and you end up feeling continually rushed and unsatisfied.

Resources

Books and Magazines

Blanke, Gail. *In My Wildest Dreams: Living the Life You Long For.* New York: Simon & Schuster, 1998.

Bliss, Edwin C. *Getting Things Done: The ABCs of Time Management.* New York: Bantam, 1995.

Booher, Dianna. *Get a Life Without Sacrificing Your Career: How to Make More Time for What's Really Important.* New York: McGraw-Hill, 1997.

Chira, Susan. *A Mother's Place: Taking the Debate About Working Mothers Beyond Guilt and Blame.* New York: HarperCollins, 1999.

Covey, Stephen R., A. Roger Merrill, and Rebecca R. Merrill. *First Things First.* New York: Simon & Schuster, 1995.

Culp, Stephanie. *Streamlining Your Life: A Five-Point Plan for Uncomplicated Living.* Cincinnati: Writer's Digest, 1991.

Davidson, Jeff. *Breathing Space: Living & Working at a Comfortable Pace in a Sped-Up Society.* New York: MasterMedia, 1991.

Douglass, Merrill E., and Donna N. Douglass. *Time Management for Teams.* New York: AMACOM, 1992.

Resources

Edwards, Paul and Sarah. *Working from Home: Everything You Need to Know About Living and Working Under the Same Roof.* New York: Putnam, 1994.

Fast Company magazine. www.fastcompany.com

Felton, Sandra. *The Messies Manual.* Grand Rapids, MI: Fleming H. Revell, 1983.

Fortgang, Laura Berman. *Intercoach News.* E-mail newsletter. lbf@intercoach.com

———. *Take Yourself to The Top: The Secrets of America's #1 Career Coach.* New York: Warner Books, 1998.

Hemphill, Barbara. *Taming the Office Tiger: The Complete Guide to Getting Organized at Work.* Washington, D.C.: Kiplinger Books, 1996.

———. *Taming the Paper Tiger: Organizing the Paper in Your Life.* Washington, D.C.: Kiplinger Books, 1997.

Home Office Computing magazine. www.smalloffice.com

Klein, Ruth. *Where Did the Time Go? A Working Woman's Guide to Creative Time Management.* Rocklin, CA: Prima Publishing, 1993.

Kolberg, Judith. *Surviving Chronic Disorganization: A Radical Guide to Getting Organized for Packrats, Clutterholics, Right-Brain Thinkers, Absent-Minded Types, Procrastinators, Perfectionists, and Adults with Learning Differences.* Audiotape with booklet. 1996. FileHeads Professional Organizers, 1142 Chatsworth Drive, Avondale Estates, GA, 30002; (404) 231-6172.

Lakein, Alan. *How to Get Control of Your Time and Your Life.* New York: New American Library, 1996.

Langhoff, June. *The Business Traveler's Survival Guide: How to Get Work Done While on the Road.* Newport, RI: Aegis Publishing, 1997.

LeBoeuf, Michael. *Working Smart: How to Accomplish More in Half the Time.* New York: Warner Books, 1993.

Levine, James A., and Todd L. Pittinsky. *Working Fathers: New Strategies for Balancing Work and Life.* Reading, MA: Addison-Wesley, 1997.

Resources

Lockwood, Georgene. *The Complete Idiot's Guide to Organizing Your Life*. New York: Alpha Books, 1996.

Lonier, Terri. *The Frugal Entrepreneur: Creative Ways to Save Time, Energy, and Money in Your Business*. New Paltz, NY: Portico Press, 1996.

————. *Working Solo: The Real Guide to Freedom and Financial Success with Your Own Business*. New York: John Wiley, 1998.

Mackenzie, Alec. *Time For Success: A Goal-Getter's Strategy*. New York: McGraw-Hill, 1991.

Mayer, Jeffrey J. *If You Haven't Got the Time to Do It Right, When Will You Find the Time to Do It Over?* New York: Simon & Schuster, 1991.

Moskowitz, Robert. *How to Organize Your Work and Your Life: Proven Time Management Techniques for Business, Professional, and Other Busy People*. San Diego: Main Street Books, 1981.

Peters, Joan K. *When Mothers Work: Loving Our Children Without Sacrificing Our Selves*. Reading, MA: Addison-Wesley, 1998.

St. James, Elaine. *Living the Simple Life: A Guide to Settling Down and Enjoying More*. New York: Hyperion, 1998.

————. *Simplify Your Life with Kids: 100 Ways to Make Family Life Easier and More Fun*. Kansas City, MO: Andrews McMeel, 1997.

Schor, Juliet B. *The Overworked American: The Unexpected Decline of Leisure*. New York: Basic Books, 1993.

Shenk, David. *Data Smog: Surviving the Information Glut*. New York: HarperCollins, 1997.

Sher, Barbara. *I Could Do Anything . . . If I Only Knew What It Was: How to Discover What You Really Want and How to Get It*. New York: Delacorte Press, 1994.

Sher, Barbara, and Annie Gottlieb, *Wishcraft: How to Get What You Really Want*. New York: Ballantine Books, 1986.

Sinetar, Marsha. *Do What You Love, the Money Will Follow: Discovering Your Right Livelihood*. Mahwah, NJ: Paulist Press, 1987.

Resources

Winston, Stephanie. *The Organized Executive, a Program for Productivity: New Ways to Manage Time, Paper, People, and the Electronic Office.* New York: Warner Books, 1994.

Services

Business Strategy Seminars
120 E. 34th Street #14-B
New York, NY 10016
212-481-7075
Support and strategy groups for small businesses.

Direct Marketing Association
212-768-7277
To reduce junk mail and telemarketers' calls by having your name removed from lists, ask about their Mail Preference and Telephone Preference Services.

Let's Talk Business Network
54 West 39th Street
12th Floor
New York, NY 10018
212-742-1553
www.LTBN.com
The nation's first entrepreneurial support network and syndicated radio show.

LifeDesigns
800-752-7314
www.lifedesigns.com
An organization whose mission is to help women define their lives and dreams.

Resources

Life On Purpose Institute
www.lifeonpurpose.com
A variety of services, including a free newsletter, for people who want to lead lives full of meaning and purpose.

Messies Anonymous
c/o Sandra Felton
5025 S.W. 114 Ave.
Miami, FL 33165
www.messies.com
Newsletter, books, and other help for chronically disorganized people.

National Association of Professional Organizers (NAPO)
1033 La Posada Drive, Suite #220
Austin, TX 78752-3880
512-206-0151
Referrals to organizing professionals nationwide.

Supplies

Everyday File & Fast Sorter (tickler file)
Globe-Weis
Available in office supply stores.

Taming the Paper Tiger Software (file index software)
The Monticello Corporation
4060 Peachtree Road
Suite D-339
Atlanta, GA 30319-3006
800-430-0794
www.thepapertiger.com

Resources

Planner Pad (appointment/planning book)
Planner Pads, Inc.
Omaha, NE
402-592-0676
Available by mail order only.

Quad Planner (appointment/planning book)
At-A-Glance Company
Sidney, NY
607-563-9411
Available in office supply stores.

Outlook 98 (scheduling, information, and contact management software)
Microsoft Corporation
Available in computer stores.

Index

About the Author

Photo by Sue Ann Miller

JAN JASPER is a productivity and time-management consultant who has worked one-on-one with clients since 1988. She is based in New York City.

For information about Jan Jasper's consulting services, seminars, and training, call 212–465–7472 or visit www.janjasper.com.